— THE —
VILLAGE

THE EARLY YEARS

=THE= VILLAGE

THE EARLY YEARS

NIGEL FARRELL

BBC BOOKS

Nigel Farrell is a radio and television producer
and presenter. His previous books include *How To Survive
Commuting* and *Fatherhood: The Awful Truth*. He lives
in Hampshire.

This book is based on the Radio 4 series of the same name which was
broadcast in 1990, 1991 and 1992. The radio series was produced by
Chris Paling and its writer and presenter was Nigel Farrell.

Published by BBC Books,
an imprint of BBC Worldwide Publishing.
BBC Worldwide Limited, Woodlands,
80 Wood Lane, London W12 0TT

First published 1992
This revised edition 1996

ISBN 0 563 38311 9

Designed by Gwyn Lewis
Map by Eugene Fleury
Illustrations by Delphine MacCormick

Set in 11pt Baskerville by Phoenix Photosetting, Chatham
Printed and bound in Great Britain by Clays Ltd, St Ives plc

For Sara Holmes

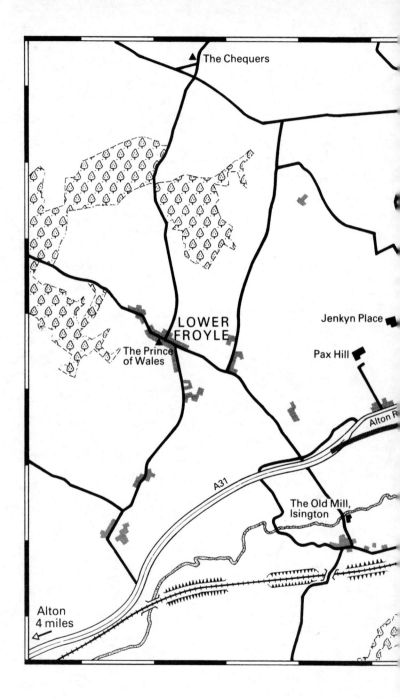

The Chequers

LOWER FROYLE

The Prince of Wales

Jenkyn Place

Pax Hill

Alton R

A31

The Old Mill, Isington

Alton
4 miles

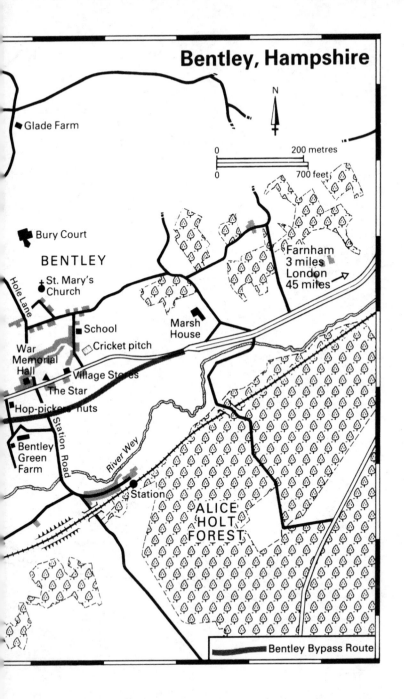

INTRODUCTION

On several occasions during the writing of this book, I have had to remind myself that Bentley is a real village, peopled not by figments of my imagination, but by real human beings. The events and conversations are related here as they really happened. Once or twice there was a temptation to play God and add a little spice, but a quick reminder that fact is indeed stranger than fiction proved that eminently resistable. After all, if you wrote a novel based on some of *The Village* storylines people would shake their heads in disbelief. The only licence I have allowed myself is to move the chronology about slightly in order to make the narrative easier to follow.

The combination of documentary and soap opera has proved a novel and often intriguing concoction. Amazingly, quite a large number of listeners and viewers believe that those who appear are actors who have actually learnt lines. Even more common is the belief that contributors are paid (no-one is paid, although the parish council have received a number of grants from the broadcasters).

So why on earth did people agree to put their heads so publicly above the parapet? Once they understood that we were not relentlessly pursuing a journalistic angle, people seemed genuinely pleased to talk about their own lives, their problems and fears and delights and, when I think about it, I suppose we all do. Much to our initial surprise, most people approached have been only too happy to help. One or two were less helpful and there's been a fair bit of muted criticism behind our backs, nearly always from those not invited to appear on the programme.

There's one question everyone who's heard or seen the programme asks: why Bentley? The answer is, no reason at all. The whole point of the experiment was to take a place, and a time, completely at random. All the normal rules of documentary making went out of the window. There was no planning, no research. I drove through Bentley one afternoon and thought this will do – a place large enough to have a bit going on, but small enough to have retained a strong sense of its own identity. It could have been any of thousands of others, for what we wanted was simply an ordinary English village, not one blighted by a nuclear power station or on the route of the Channel Tunnel Rail Link. The first person I met in Bentley was Tony Holmes, and since he and his family were brave enough to allow me to start with them, that's what we did, there and then.

What began life as a series of six fifteen-minute radio programmes became nearly fifty episodes on Radio 4 and subsequently forty-two half-hour episodes (to date) on television. Everyone involved, including – or perhaps especially – me, has been astonished by the programme's popularity. It seems to have struck a chord in a public that has clearly grown tired of a relentless diet of documentaries about murder, rape, child abuse and incest.

This book covers the early years of the programme which gave birth to many of the story lines which are still running today. The passage of time is one subject radio and television are not good at covering, and an unexpected bonus to *The Village* has been observing the characters we've got to know and love grow old. I don't know of any other programme that has ever enjoyed the luxury of following the day-to-day lives of people over such a long period. Incredibly, we started work on the first programme seven years ago, and in the duration we've watched people grow up, fall in love, have children, retire, die - this after all was always intended to be the real world, where life goes on and rarely falls into the convenient beginnings, middles and ends so beloved by programme-makers.

Over the years I have grown to know Bentley as well as many of the people whose families have lived there for generations and, each time I come away from it, I am moved by the warmth, hospitality and generosity of spirit I have received. Its people have indeed charmed us all, and I'm sure we're the better for it.

═ ONE ═

'Give 'em room, they've got to have room to show themselves. Give 'em room to be admired, to walk on and then stand with legs well apart, so you can see their shape. Give 'em room, I say, give 'em room!'

Tony Holmes, propped up by a great knobbly walking-stick, was leaning keenly over the rope of the showring, scrutinizing each of the huge Romagnola bulls as one by one they lumbered forward for inspection by the judges.

'Give him room, Bob,' he shouted across to his cattleman. 'Show him off!'

This was the Royal Show at Stoneleigh, the most exhilarating day of Tony's calendar, a chance for the pride of Glade Farm's prize-winning herd to reap the honours he'd dreamed of all year. His glowing, ruddy face, topped by a shaggy mop of grey hair, had for once lost its huge, whiskery smile.

'Those two there, they ought to part them, give 'em room, that's no damn good, let 'em stride on like a good 'un – put his legs together, man, so he'll flatten out his back! Hey, Bob, give him room!'

A hundred yards away, at the other end of the cluster of cattle arenas, Tony's wife Sara was deep in passionate debate over the finer points of another breed, her own beloved Belted Galloways. This was the ultimate indulgence in the cattle-breeding world: husband and wife, each with their own individual herd, competing against all comers and each other for the coveted cups they each hoped would take pride of place on the mantelpiece at Glade Farm.

'It's the sheer thrill of the thing, isn't it, Campbell?' said Sara, with a keen religious zeal. 'The thrill of the unexpected, you see. You get two or three years of nothing but runts, then the following year, jiminy-cricket, you get a crop of absolute corkers!'

The talk is of nothing but Belties and Romagnolas from dawn till dusk. They stand in small, animated groups, only stopping for breath when the judge makes his announcement.

'It's like human beings – two beautiful people don't necessarily produce a beautiful child, they more than likely have a Plain Jane.' Sara was still in full flood, her tall figure an elegant splash of colour beside the grey trilbies and gumboots of the men clustered dutifully around her. Her voice, resonant in its mastery of the subject, rose above the groans of the cattle, frequently disintegrating into peals of raucous laughter.

'Two beautiful 'umans normally produce little pests,' said Campbell, with real feeling. His father had won the Belted Galloway Best In Class Bowl three years running back in the thirties, and in celebration he'd had his baby son christened in the trophy itself. 'Belties in me blood,' Campbell always said.

'And sometimes the Plain Janes produce the most absolutely corking calves,' added Sara, suddenly poking him in the ribs.

'Look out, here comes Snoops,' she announced, as her favourite Beltie was led hesitantly into the showring. 'Give 'em what for, Snoops!'

Glade Farm is a large, modern farmhouse overlooking the village of Bentley. It was built by Tony's father Captain Dick Holmes high on a sloping field opposite a little terraced row of farmworkers' cottages at the top of Hole Lane. Captain Holmes knew what he was doing – Glade House has breathtaking views over the 2000 acres of rolling North Hampshire countryside now farmed by Tony and Sara, and which run down to the village in the valley below. Sixty years ago, those fields were given over entirely to the crop which made this corner of Hampshire one of the wealthiest in the South of England – hops. Old Captain Holmes was the biggest landowner in the area, so it came as no surprise to the village when in 1933 he formed a partnership with a very successful local hop-merchant, Bob Pike.

The two families were close; Captain Holmes' son, Tony, became friends with Bob's young son, Mike. When eventually Tony decided to marry, he naturally asked Mike to be an usher at the wedding, held, like his father's before him, in the lovely twelfth-century church of St Mary's down below Glade Farm; and when Mike in turn fell in love with an eye-catching young girl called Sara, who else should he ask to be an usher but Tony Holmes? Then, by a bizarre twist of fate, both families were thrown into disarray by two appalling tragedies which came hard on the heels of one another. In January 1972, Sara's husband Mike, an apparently healthy man in his mid-thirties, went out jogging one morning and never returned – he was found dead from a heart attack. Then on Guy Fawkes' Night that same year, Tony's wife and daughter were killed in a car accident whilst driving to a bonfire party along the notorious Alton-Farnham road.

As time went by, the widow and widower, old friends anyway, found themselves drawn together. Tony, with one surviving son, Chris, and Sara, with two young daughters, Pom and Sally, eventually decided to marry, and together the new and considerably enlarged family set up home in Glade Farm. Sara produced another daughter, Fogs, and began to plan the development of her Beltie herd; Tony set about trying to reverse the decline in his hop sales and developing his Romagnola herd; and down in the valley below, the villagers wondered at the strange way in which the families of the two great local farming dynasties had become one.

To see them together now, waving, grinning, blowing raspberries at each other from either end of the Royal Show cattle enclosure, no one could have guessed the suffering that had gone before, and no one could have imagined a happier pair, gambolling about like teenagers amidst the mud and steam of the rows of snorting cattle.

'Good luck, darling!' waved Sara from her arena, and Tony waved back frantically with his stick.

On the other side of Hole Lane, opposite Glade Farm, Tony's son Chris emerged from one of the old farmworker's cottages where he now lives, and paused for a moment in the summer sunshine considering how best to spend the rest of the day. With his father away, he relished a few days alone and in charge of the farm, despite some of the farmhands muttering darkly about his youth and inexperience, just as they had when Tony took over from the Captain.

Every other farm in the area has long since given up growing hops, but somehow Glade Farm has managed to retain sixty acres, and with it a tradition and a way of life that goes back centuries. Soon the hop-pickers would start arriving, just as they had at the end of every summer for generations. It was time to check what needed doing to the little whitewashed huts where the pickers lived for the harvest. Last year they had promised to install electricity, Chris reminded himself a little guiltily, before jumping into the dusty red Citroen van marked 'Vin Rouge' and shooting off down the narrow lane.

At last an elderly gent with a long waxed moustache and gleaming bowler hat stepped into the centre of the show ring and started to write down the list of winners. Tony's cattleman Bob Bates, his white coat spattered with mud, stood nervously beside the bull, but Tony himself, hunched over the stick, seemed in buoyant mood. 'Call that a flat back!' he chortled at one of his competitors. 'Give him room, man, let him walk on. You'll never win a thing if you don't let him walk on. Treat him like a good woman!'

The judge's assistant started holding up the numbers of the winning bulls. Tony craned forward. 'Now, what have we got . . . not one . . . not two . . .'

For a moment he seemed to be struggling to control his expression. 'Not two . . . what have we got . . . not three . . .'

'I've lost my spectacles,' said a little old lady standing beside him, 'I can't see what position you've got Tony . . . is it a first?'

Suddenly, for the first time that afternoon, Tony seemed lost for words, as a look of total disbelief crossed his face.

'One . . . two . . . three . . . four . . .' Tony slowly retraced the order. 'Four . . . five . . . we came fifth.'

'Out of how many?'

'Five.'

It didn't take long for Tony, ever stoical, to regain his composure.

'Ah well.' he said. 'That is life. That . . . is . . . life!'

The pickers' sheds made an incongruous little whitewashed terrace in the middle of a field on the other side of the main road. After inspecting them and making a mental note to install electricity in time for next year's picking instead, Chris crossed over to meet Brian Wilkins, in charge of the huge shed which houses the hop-picking machine. Together the two men inspected the rows of young vines nearby which even now were reaching like great bushy fingers to the tops of the trelliswork.

'We're going to have to harvest early, Brian, if the red spider's not to have a field day.'

'What we need is a bit of rain to wash the little perishers away.'

Sixty years ago, nigh on two thousand travellers would have descended on Bentley for hop-picking in late August. At the busiest weekends the main road was actually closed to traffic to allow the hundreds of thirsty workers to spill out of the village's two main pubs, the Star and the Red Lion, and to allow plenty of room for spectators to enjoy the endless drunken brawls between the city folk and the local boys.

Today the Red Lion has long since closed, but there's still work on Glade Farm for a handful of pickers, and some of them, faces sooty with dust and hop-leaves hanging from the back of their collars, can still be seen in the Star, whilst other local pubs, by sheer force of habit, put out the traditional blackboards with the words 'No Travellers' scrawled across in chalk, even though they haven't seen a picker for years.

The dreaded red spider mite, scarcely visible to the naked eye, thrives in dry heat. In the old days the pesticides would knock them stone dead, but now so many types are banned that the red spider had returned with a vengeance, depositing thousands of its eggs in the vines. These thrive by sucking more and more moisture from the growing stems, until the entire crop withers.

As soon as Tony and Sara had returned trophyless from the Royal Show and Bob Bates had passed the message up from the sheds at Bury Court that all the cattle had been successfully unloaded, the company of Holmes, Holmes & Son held an emergency session over mugs of coffee in the big kitchen of Glade House.

'We're going to have to bring things forward at least a couple of weeks if we're not to lose the lot,' Chris said, not so much asking permission as announcing a decision.

'Can we get the message out to the troops in time?' asked Tony. 'Ada and the rest are booked in at the end of the month, aren't they? And what does Brian say?'

Their sixty acres of hops are still more profitable to Glade Farm than the rest of the 1900 acres of farmland put together. Unlike many of the other local producers, Tony had developed a hop which seemed to suit lager production, and he'd struck a deal to see Glade Farm at least through the next three years.

'After then, who knows?' he said. 'It's so sad, what's happening to beer these days. It's a rich man's drink, when you compare it to the price of a glass of whisky. And besides that, it's part of the character of the place. If we didn't have those sixty acres, we'd be sacking three men. Living in a village like this and you sack three men, you're the biggest so-and-so in Christendom, and I'd know how they felt. Oh no, it'll be a sad day when there's no hops grown down Bentley way.'

That evening, among the long shadows in the hop-gardens below Glade Farm, squadrons of swallows dived and swirled in and out of the vines, searching for greenfly. 'That's the pickers' omen for a good harvest,' said Tony wistfully, 'And damn the red spider!'

In a tiny maisonette on a vast concrete sixties estate at Manor Park, in the East End of London, Ada Allen put down the telephone and allowed herself the luxury of a triumphant smile. She'd be travelling down to Bentley nearly three weeks earlier than planned, and the thought of it gave her an exquisite thrill. Her grandparents had been hop-pickers, and so had her parents, and now here she was, sixty-eight and bowed by arthritis, about to go on the annual pilgrimage yet again, with her grandson Chris in his battered old Cortina to drive her down.

'It's Christmas I first start thinking about it. I dream of the warmth and the friends and the smell of the things, it's lovely. Then it's Easter, and I think they'll soon be trainin' the hops, and then I 'phone up Tony and Sara, lovely people, lovely family, and every year I'm still surprised when Tony says he still wants me. I'm lonely here,' she said, waving a shaky hand towards the little mantelpiece with its neat row of family photos and the faces she so rarely saw these days. Outside the wail of a police-car siren momentarily drowned the endless groan of the traffic.

'If you're not a picker you'll never understand. I'd love to live down there. I've asked Tony time and time again to find me a place down there, but now I'm ready for the knacker's yard, it's too late. I think my life would end the day Tony said I couldn't come hop-picking, I do really, I'd die. It'd be a bad day for me.'

And with that, she suddenly remembered the early summons, and excitedly rang her grandson Chris to pass on the news, and check he could come down with her. Of course he could, he'd be round nine sharp on Saturday.

Before she went to bed that night, Ada went to the back of her wardrobe and pulled out a dusty old tilly-lamp which dated from before the last war, and a can of oil. She and Chris would be needing that, over the next few weeks.

═ TWO ═

Sara buzzed about the dusty hop-shed, clipboard and papers in one hand, slapping them on the shoulders or shaking their hands with the other, her ramrod-straight deportment giving her an air of royal breeding, her face beaming with the sheer pleasure of the occasion.

'Hello Ethel, dear, how are you? I'm sorry Albert can't make it this year . . . hello Tim, how are the twins? Four years old already? I remember them being born, talk about panic stations, seems like only yester-day . . .'

It was only seven-thirty in the morning, yet the place hummed with a sense of celebration. From London, Reading, Southampton and Basingstoke they'd come – the hop-pickers. The women stood waiting beside the vast, slumbering old hop-picking machine where they'd spend most of the next few weeks, waiting to greet Sara and sign on with her.

She'd done the men before seven, and now they were out in the fields, loading up the tractors and trailers which would arrive in the shed every ten minutes, throwing up huge clouds of dust before dropping their load into the hungry machine and roaring off.

'Make sure you turn up every morning, or you don't get your money for the previous day's work . . . there's method to my madness,' said Sara, with a giggle, to two newcomers. This was her job, no one else's, and she did it with the enjoyment and pride of a much-loved ritual, the older pickers smiling with her as she worked her way around the line. For them, like her, harvesting the hops had never just been a question of money; more part of the pattern of the seasons, as certain as summer, and as welcome.

Then, suddenly, there was Ada, hobbling in from the sunlight. Sara moved straight across to her, and for a moment the two women stood, perhaps wanting to embrace, but aware of the class barriers that separated them. They shared a mutual respect for each other borne of many summers' work together.

'Another year, I can't believe it, Ada, I can't believe it,' said Sara.

'You still 'appy to have me, Mrs Holmes? I'm not far off the knacker's yard, you know!'

'Nonsense!' replied Sara with a snort, and for a few minutes the proceedings halted whilst the two old friends started to catch up on twelve months of family news.

The machine took up most of the shed, and looked to the newcomers like some ramshackle, sprawling antique that should have been confined long ago to an agricultural museum, were there ever one large enough to accommodate it. It had probably only survived because the cost of replacing it would have put the farm out of business overnight. Once the vines are dropped

Hop-pickers' huts

from the tractors, they're thrown up by one of the more muscular farmhands on to huge moving hooks which then feed them into the great wheezing bowels of the machine. The buds are shorn off and sent scuttling down onto a twisting conveyor-line, the stems and leaves shredded and blown out behind the shed onto a vast mountain of chaff which by the end of harvest would grow higher than the shed itself.

Ada sat all day on her special cushion on a built-in seat, picking out any mouldy buds and throwing them into sacks, haloed by a cloud of dust, vibrating with the deafening sound of the machine.

'Back home, back in E12, they think I'm loopy to come down 'ere and do this, but to me its 'eaven, they don't understand, you see.' At lunch, they help her over the main road, into the hut she shares with her grandson Chris, and then all afternoon she's back on her seat, until five, when the working day ends, and she makes Chris his supper over the little gas stove.

Sometimes Chris and the younger ones make a fire, and sit talking into the early hours, and she dozes, exhausted, in the darkness.

In the next hut were Rita and Jen, both packers for Harrods of London and, like Ada, both adamant that while others may favour Blackpool or the Costa del Sol, for them Tony's hop-gardens are the only conceivable place on earth to be in August.

'We just finished packing a three-piece suite for some of them Sheiks before we came away,' Rita was telling Ada. 'Fourteen thousand pounds, it cost, and it makes you sick, doesn't it?' Ada nodded, wide-eyed. 'Mind you, Ade, last week we packed off a china cup and saucer to a gentleman in Japan. Two hundred and fifty pounds! Just for a cup of tea – teabag extra, mind!'

'Glad you made it, though, Reet.'

'Nothing changes down here in Bentley, does it? Up in Town they're dropping off at fifty or sixty, but here, it's nothing to see eighty and ninety-year-olds. Its slower, you see, just the same one year as the next. Life passes Bentley by, don't it Ade?'

In charge of the hop-picking shed was Tony's first lieutenant, Brian Wilkins, his slight, oil-stained figure to be found darting endlessly in and out of the dark shadows of his great machine, working hard to avoid the nightmare of a breakdown. Last year they'd lost two days because of a burst sump, and Tony had not let him forget it. It was Brian's finger pressing the big red button that got the machine groaning and heaving into action, and it was Brian who chased and chivvied his girls to drink up after tea-break.

'Ready to go again, girls? Chop-chop!'

'Ready, willing and able,' said Ada, with a twinkle.

'That's nice to know!'

'See what I mean, Eth? But 'e's a lovely man. 'E'll be pushing me in 'ere in me geriatric bed!'

'You watch 'is hands, Ade!'

Sara jumped into the Range-Rover, with its miniature silver Belted Galloway gleaming on the front of the bonnet, and with a wave at Brian, shot off down the yard and nosed out into the heavy morning traffic of the main road. There had been plans for a bypass for Bentley for fifty years, and now once again there were signs that soon work on it might really be getting under way. Tony, as chairman of the parish council, had been told to call an open meeting. Soon Ministry men in bright orange anoraks had appeared again all over the Holmes' land with tripods and theodolites slung over their shoulders.

The old road was one of the main routes linking London with Portsmouth and Southampton. Five miles east of the village is Farnham, with the old coaching inns of the Bush Hotel and the Nelson's Arms, built opposite the great house where his Lordship, en route to the Fleet and immortality, would have a final night of passion with Lady Hamilton. Five miles to the west lie Alton and the magnificent hills and dales of the Meon Valley, rolling down to the Solent and the distant outline of the Isle of Wight.

Beside the road runs the Wey, which rises in Alton, weaves past Bentley and on through Surrey to join the Thames. When Tony and Sara were first married, the hounds of the otter hunt made an annual visit, and the river frequently burst its banks, but now it's often reduced to nothing more than a trickle, thanks to the gigantic steel pipes upstream which suck away millions of gallons to quench the thirst of the grey, ever-expanding sprawl of Basingstoke to the north.

On the other side of the river stands the little community of houses surrounding a tiny, idyllic Victorian station, with its single track running to the end of the line at Alton. In the fifties and sixties cohorts of birdwatchers from London would sit for hours in their specially chartered train carriages listening to the dusk chorus of the nightingales in the nearby woods, the beginning of the great Alice Holt forest which covers the southern side of the valley. That is probably what gave rise to the name Bentley, which means 'green by the forest'. The new bypass would run between the station and the river, slicing off the station from the rest of the village.

At the crossroads by the War Memorial Hall, Sara turned right leaving the Star and the village shop behind, and drove up Hole Lane, past the surgery and the quaintly-named Babs Field council estate, on up past Jenkyn Place and the church, eventually turning right into the steep drive of Glade House.

'Who is Mrs Joyce anyway, when she's at home?' demanded Tony, leaning on a corner of the kitchen table. Maureen picked up the great steaming mug of coffee from the hob, negotiated carefully past a vast bean-bag squashed flat by a heap of snoring dogs and placed it down in front of him.

'She's the Health Visitor. Apparently there's been another baby born like my Catherine, and she wants me to talk to the mother, to tell her the treatment can work, that its not a lost cause.'

'Good for you, you tell her.'

Fourteen years ago, when Sara moved in to Glade House with Tony, and their daughter Fogs was born,

Maureen had offered to come up and help run the house; she's been doing it ever since, although she always tries to leave by midday so she can continue to help cook dinners down at the school. Eventually when one of the terraced farm cottages opposite Glade House became vacant, Tony offered it to Maureen and her husband, and the bond between Maureen and the family grew even stronger, even though she still always insists on referring to Tony and Sara as 'Mr and Mrs Holmes'.

A couple of years later, Maureen had a daughter herself, Catherine, and the circumstances surrounding her extraordinary birth made the child something of a village legend. She was born two months prematurely, and much to the astonishment of the medical staff, the baby had appeared with her bowel and intestines outside the body. At first they assumed she would die, but over the months the experts at Great Ormond Street hospital had painstakingly repaired her, and after a time Catherine began to thrive. 'Not that you'd know there'd been a thing wrong, not when you look at her now,' Tony always said, when Maureen brought Catherine up to Glade House with her during the school holidays.

'What about the belly-button, any news on that?' he asked.

'We're trying to get in touch with a plastic surgeon again, to see if they can make a belly-button. These short tops are all the rage now – '

'Don't I know it – '

'But Catherine's embarrassed to wear one.'

'I suppose it must look a bid odd, just a blank space.'

'Apparently they take some skin from somewhere

else and serrate it, like a tomato in a salad, and they reckon it'll look very realistic.'

'Extraordinary business,' said Tony, shaking his head and taking a gulp of coffee.

The week before there had been a call from *Woman's Own* magazine, and Maureen suddenly found she had agreed to let herself and Catherine be photographed, and the whole story written up.

'You nervous then?'

'I only agreed because they said it would help the others, Mr Holmes. I think Catherine's quite excited, she likes the idea of the fame, but I'm terrified.'

'Nonsense, woman, you'll be great.'

'I don't know what they'll say about it, down in the village.'

Out in the fields, the sun shone as it had relentlessly for weeks, and at last the men turned off the tractor, shook the leaves from their hair and coats, and sat slumped in the shade, ready for a tea-break.

They were a motley gang, as always, but this year far fewer in number. Tony was experimenting with a new vine-pulling machine, and it was working well: instead of half-a-dozen men clambering up ladders and tearing down the vines by hand, large motorised wheels were mounted on the back of the tractors, and with these taking the strain of the pulling, only three men were required on each wheel to feed in the vines. The great scenes of Tony's childhood, when hundreds of men swarmed around the hop-gardens like locusts, were gone forever.

'Here, boys, have a swig of this and moisten your throats,' said George Cowdray, the foreman, offering a mug to two drained-looking Eton schoolboys who'd spent most of the morning wheezing, sneezing and scratching, in the dust from the vines.

'We had those Portuguese and Eyeties here last year, and that group of doctors, but there'd be no room for them now, not even if they came. How are you feeling, Taff?'

Taff was a swarthy-looking Welshman who'd turned up unannounced the previous day after hiking all the way from the Welsh valleys, and Sara had felt she had to enrol him.

'Wrists and shoulders a bit sore, but nothing a few pints won't sort out tonight,' said Taff. His dark face was pitted with blotches of dried blood from the scratches of the raw stems of the vines, a sure sign that he'd not picked before.

A tractor pulled up, and out jumped Ada's grand-son Chris, blonde hair down to his shoulders, and with the kind of bouncy energy only the drivers could summon up by this stage in the day. Ada had been bringing Chris to Glade Farm since he was in a pram, and this year Brian Wilkins had rewarded his years of loyalty and dedication by giving him his own tractor, and with it a status that commanded the immediate respect of the other pickers.

For the rest of the year, Chris worked at a car paint-sprayer's yard in Stratford, E11, where he spent all day, every day, in a corrugated tin hut behind a disused garage wearing goggles and face-mask and encased in a toxic, multicoloured mist.

'Are you here for the month?' asked George.

'Sure,' said Chris. 'Think I'm in a hurry to get back?'

'But you only get a fortnight's summer holiday.'

'That's right,' said Chris, with a smile. 'And a very long fortnight it can sometimes turn out to be, too.'

Down in the old room beneath the drying kiln, with its low, bowed wooden ceiling and ancient woodblock floor, Ada and Rita were sharing a mug of coffee and planning the party. It was too noisy to talk when the machine was going.

'Tony's got a generator we can have, and Brian's dug up some coloured lights, bless 'im,' said Ada. Every year, the pickers played host to the farm-hands, frying a ton of sausages and beans over an open fire, and providing as much beer and cider as the men could drink.

'What about music, Ade?'

'Chris has brought his new Pavarotti tapes.'

'Blimey,' said Rita.

'Hello, Patricia, how lovely to see you.'

Sara lent forward and kissed her old friend resolutely on the cheek.

'Oh, how nice to see you both, come in, have a sherry,' said Mrs Coke, with obvious pleasure. She pottered off down the huge hall and into the drawing-room, then stood beside the great French windows, looking down at the gardens basking in the late afternoon sunshine. Far below were the hop-gardens.

Mrs Patricia Coke, of Jenkyn Place, is slight and very elegant. Her smile still has a delight and a charm, her manner is easy and confident. Her father was the Hon. Sir Alexander Cadogan, O.M., who had been Permanent Under-Secretary at the Foreign Office throughout the War, responsible for implementing Britain's foreign policy at one of the most critical periods in her history. Her great-grandmother was German, and married the Duke of Manchester, before later running off with the Duke of Devonshire, to become a Duchess for the second time. 'Rather unusual for a German girl to work her way through two English Dukes in succession,' Mrs Coke would say. 'She must have been quite a girl.'

'I'm longing to hear all about it, Tony, the harvest, I mean. The gardens have been superb, we've never had so much flower on everything. It's quite wonderful.'

'You've not been suffering from the drought, then, like us?'

'Well, not too badly, you know, we've had lots of manure, courtesy of your lovely Belties, thank goodness. Can you smell the limes?' she asked, swinging open the window. 'They've been absolutely full of honey-bees today. Gerald always used to say that there's something about the air around here, don't you think? It's the first real village as you come out of London, isn't it, as you come over the Surrey border and enter Hampshire, you're in the country, aren't you, and the air smells so different.'

For a moment all their thoughts returned to Gerald, who had been so much a part of the village for fifty years, and who had died so suddenly at New Year. The gardens had been his creation.

'Now, tell me about this blessed red spider,' said Mrs Coke, at last.

'Never mind the blessed red spider, it's all these blessed EEC directives,' said Sara. 'Not allowed to spray the modern chemicals anymore. We'll be back to using Jeyes Fluid, if we're not careful,' she added. 'Just like we did before the War.'

'What we really need is a hard winter,' said Tony. 'That would do us all good.'

Down in the hop-shed, beyond the hop-gardens that lie below the luxurious southern lawns of Jenkyn Place, Brian Wilkins suddenly felt a moment of panic.

The machine had stopped. He ran around to the front of the shed. A group of women had gathered at the top of the running-belt.

'What's happened?'

Rita came hurrying towards him.

'Get the doctor, Brian. Quick.'

'What's happened?'

'Quick, Brian. It's Ada. She's gone grey. I think she's had a heart-attack.'

THREE

In the early spring of 1941 Gerald Coke brought his beautiful young bride Patricia down from London to their new home at Jenkyn Place. Of course, the gardens were nothing then. This was the time of 'Dig for Victory', so the Cokes set about growing tons of fruit and vegetables where now there are stunning vistas of hybrid teas and narcissi; cattle roamed the lower part of the gardens, and the lawns went for hay.

The bulk of the present house, with its distinctive dormer windows set in a steep sloping roof above the imposing frontage, was built on the site of old farm buildings in 1687. Under the hallway is the ancient Jancknes's Well; for centuries those travelling the Pilgrim's Way, which led by the shortest route from church to church from Winchester to Canterbury, paused here between Froyle Church and Bentley Church, to drink at the well and throw in a coin for luck on their journey.

The Cokes set about renovating their new acquisition, which after the war gradually began again to look like the fine example of a seventeenth century English country house it once had been. At the same time they promoted one of their bright young junior gardeners, Walter Sherfield, who had been working at Jenkyn Place since 1931, to Head Gardener, and together the three of them began creating Gerald's dream: a garden that one day would attract visitors from all over the world.

Over the years the Cokes and Walter watched their plants and shrubs thrive in the rich greensand soil, and soon the gardens, coddled in the warmth and protection offered by their position on the north side of the Wey Valley, grew in beauty and stature. Gerald's career prospered to such an extent that he was regarded with awe by many of the villagers: a banker with Warburg's, he became an internationally acknowledged expert on music and porcelain, a director of the Royal Opera House and a Governor of the BBC.

One morning in his eighty-third year, having planned a morning shopping trip with his wife, Gerald Coke got out of bed, went to the bathroom, and, having had not the slightest warning that anything was wrong, died within minutes of a sudden malfunction of the heart. Suddenly, after almost exactly fifty years, Patricia found herself in charge of the house, and its gardens, and quite alone.

A few days later the great cedar on the east front, planted in 1823 and one of the largest in the country, came crashing down in a storm.

'Nobody could quite believe it,' said Walter Sherfield, living in retirement in his cottage in Toad Hole Lane, a few yards from the gate of Jenkyn Place. 'It was so sudden, see, and there was something ominous in

that great tree a-comin' down so soon after he died. Mr Coke would have been desolate, had he known that.'

Walter had worked at Jenkyn Place for almost half a century, and even now, at eighty-two, still dapper in his tie and fresh white collar, always helped out when needed. They had summoned him for advice, of course, over the damage left by the fallen cedar; and on busy summer weekends, he and his wife Jessie would be there to hand out tickets to the scores of visitors who came from so far and wide to see the results of his labours.

'It was very frightening, Mr Holmes, very frightening indeed. Joan called out "Mum, it's Ada!" and there she was, all grey and stiff and groaning about dreadful pains in her chest, so Brian called the doctor, and 'e took 'er down to his lovely little cottage at the end of the lane – '

'VIP treatment, then – '

Jenkyn Place

'And they took 'er to Basingstoke and said, yes, it was a mild heart attack, and they've admitted her, but it was all very frightening, 'cos to us you're out in the wilds 'ere, back home you just have to pop around the corner and there's the doctor and the 'ospital, on yer doorstep, thank God she's all right, although she's very upset 'cos she's missing out on all the 'opping – '

'She can talk all right, then?' asked Tony.

'Talk? She wouldn't stop talking. The doctors had to tell 'er to shut up, they couldn't stop 'er.' Tony and the others burst into laughter, partly because they knew Ada so well, but also from a sense of relief that she was all right.

'She won't make the party, then?'

'She says she will.'

'Don't be daft.'

'You comin' on Saturday, Mr Holmes?'

'We'll do our best, Rita, but it's the South of England show, and Sara has high hopes for Petronella.'

Up at St Mary's, the beautiful twelfth century church that the pilgrims would have just been able to see ahead as they set off after making their wishes at Jenkyn Place, the huge bearded figure of the Reverend Bill Rogers was ending the usual Thursday morning service.

You could tell just by looking that it was the Thursday service because there were only six people – all women – in the congregation. On Sundays, the church is packed: St Mary's, Bentley, has the highest church attendance per head of population in the diocese of Winchester.

'Ah, Mrs Pike, how are you?' said Mr Rogers to the first in the small queue of ladies waiting to pay their respects to him before leaving. The vicar's frame blotted out almost all the daylight from the large Norman arch of the main doorway. 'This is a remarkable service, isn't it, with half the total congregation, three ladies, all having the surname Pike, and all coming from different families, too.'

'Lovely service, Mr Rogers, thank you,' said the first Mrs Pike, pottering off down the cobbled pathway which leads out under the arch of a vast old yew, twisted and bent nearly double after four centuries, now propped up by two thick oak supporting posts and forming a canopy over much of the churchyard.

'Ah, Mrs Pike, how are you?' he asked the next lady, Jean Pike, who was Sara Holmes' first mother-in-law. 'I'm the only person I know with two mothers-in-law in the same village,' Sara used to joke. 'Can get jolly complicated.'

'You always ask me how I am, Bill, and I always reply the same. I'm all right, I'm fine,' said the second Mrs Pike.

'Good morning, Lady Pike,' continued Mr Rogers, gamely working his way down the queue. 'How's Sir William?'

'Well, not too good, I'm afraid. He's got this very tiresome ear, and he's got to go into the Cambridge to have it sorted out.'

Lieutenant-General Sir William Pike was a veteran of the Royal Artillery and president of the village Fête and Flower show.

'Nasty, ear problems.'

'Well, it's too near the brain. I remember my mother saying that it always hurts nearer the brain, but since I never thought I had much brain, I took no notice.'

'Give him my best wishes. Goodbye! Ah, Mrs Collins, now you're very distinguished today, aren't you, on account of not being called Pike. All well, I trust?'

After he had finished his duties at the church, Mr Rogers set off at a brisk pace down Church Lane, turning right into Toad Hole Lane to keep his appointment with old Walter Sherfield.

' "I took up church bell-ringing in 1942," ' said old Walter, clearing his throat.

'That's it, 1942 – ' confirmed Jessie.

' "Jessie and I travelled around a bit, ringing in several towers. We was always made welcome in all towers. We went to Burton Bradstock and in an eight-bell tower at Tenby, South Wales – " '

'That's it, eight bells – '

' "Where I lost Jessie – " '

'That's right, that's where you lost me,' said Jessie, with a chuckle.

Walter and Jessie Sherfield were carefully checking old Walter's monthly column for the parish magazine, 'My Life And Times in Bentley', which began with the old man's birth in the village in 1908, and continued with his leaving school in 1922, being invalided out of the Navy, starting work at Jenkyn Place in 1931, and through to his retirement in 1978. For this issue he'd reached 1942, and his appointment as Captain of the Bells up at St Mary's, a post he proudly held for forty years.

'I hadn't got a clue where you'd got to, Walt, had I?' Jessie was almost crying with laughter.

'I went up to the tower, and you didn't know, and the curate had to set you straight. Anyway, where was I? Ah yes. "To be continued."'

'That's it, it's to be continued.'

Just then the bell rang, and the shadow of Mr Rogers fell across the doorway.

'How's my top columnist today? Made the deadline?'

'Hello, Bill, come in.'

'Got it finished?'

'Just about.'

'You know how popular it's become, don't you?'

'I was wondering about including the Tom Neal story this month.'

'Yes?' Without further prompting, Walter launched into his story.

'One day old Tom, who lived at Somerset Cottages, he liked his Sunday pre-lunch drink at the old Red Lion, as it was then. He came out at two o'clock, and he rolled along out onto the doorstep and down to the cobblestones, at it was then, just as our rector at the time, Reverend Moody, was passing by. He called out, "Drunk again, Neal!", and old Tom replies, quick as a flash, "Yes, Moody, so am I!"'

The Reverened Rogers let out a long, low chuckle.

'I'm not sure we can include that in the parish magazine, Walter,' he said, after much thought.

The distorted sound of Pavarotti groaning away in the darkness outside the hop-pickers' huts could be heard on the other side of the village.

'Who's going to eat all them sausages, Reet?' asked Chris, eyeing a charred mountain of pork that was still sizzling away merrily at the edge of the blazing fire.

'Where is everybody?'

'George, Taff and some of the others are down the Bull, busy getting tanked up, they'll be here soon.'

'Brian should be 'ere.'

'Tony said 'e'd come.'

'Bob and Jan are down the hospital. They should be 'ere soon, too.'

Bob was Ada's son, who had come down by train as soon as he heard about the heart attack. Ada's absence left a strange air of melancholy over the proceedings. The hospital had been running tests on her over the last two days, and no one at Bentley had yet heard the results. It seemed wrong to be celebrating.

Chris had hung a line of coloured lights from the wooden roofs of the old whitewashed huts, and put 'Che Faro Senza Euridice' on at full volume to drown the chatter of the old generator Brian had given them. The fields around them were translucent in the glow of the full harvest moon, and in the distance were the fierce beams of the cars on the main road, racing past the gentle, dimmer lights of the village.

'What about Ada's other children? They coming?'

'Geraldine's in Germany, then there's one in Cornwall, and another daughter – '

'They're not speaking,' said Chris.

'So it's really only Bob who can help.'

'Why hasn't Tony ever given 'er a place down 'ere? Surely there'd be a cottage free one day. It'd make 'er so 'appy.'

'Tony's told Brian he's not so sure it would make her happy, not at her age.'

Suddenly there were shouts from away in the darkness. The faces of Bob and Jan emerged, grinning, from the shadows.

'She's coming home tomorrow,' announced Jan, and the little group of pickers around the fire gave a cheer. 'She still looks a bit ashen, but they've said she's fine, they've got all her tablets and spray ready. We can pick her up at ten o'clock tomorrow morning, and we'll take her back to Manor Park.'

'She'll still be back, next year, she says, even if they have to carry her down,' said Bob.

'That's providing she does as she's told. Which is not very often, is it, Reet?'

'No,' said Rita, to a chorus of laughter.

'You'll be home next week, Chris?'

'Not unless she needs me. I'm going to tell the boss I'm off sick.'

'Yeah, you do that.'

Suddenly the boys from the Bull arrived, Pavarotti lurched into 'Donna Non Vidi Mai', and the small heap of empty beer and cider bottles started to grow rapidly.

A few minutes later another shadowy figure appeared from the darkness. This time it was Brian Wilkins, flustered and out of breath.

'What is it, Brian?'

'It's Tony Holmes. He's been knocked over by a bull at the Newbury Show.'

'Is he hurt?'

'He's in hospital, with two broken ribs and a broken ankle.' He paused for a moment, drawing breath in the chill night air.

'Mrs Holmes says he's lucky to be alive.'

FOUR

The rains started in the early hours, surprising everyone except old Walter Sherfield. By mid-morning,
the black, rolling clouds had all but obliterated the view
of Alice Holt forest at the southern limit of the valley, and
the water had formed a small river running down School
Lane, pouring onto the green so that the cricket pitch
looked like a small reservoir. Even the pigeons dared not
land on it for fear of drowning.

'Knew it was coming last night,' said Walter. 'Our
cottage here in Toad Hole Lane is about a mile up from
the railway line, and if of an evening you can hear those
trains a-rattlin' down from Bentley to Alton, you can be
sure as eggs is eggs it'll rain in the morning. Yesterday
evening the rattlin' was fair deafening.'

From the window of the drawing-room at Glade
Farm, Tony Holmes looked down into the dismal grey
of the valley.

'Too ruddy late to knock the red spider on the
head, damn it,' he said. There was a knock on the door,
and in came Maureen armed with two mugs of coffee,

one for Tony, the other for Sara, who was poring over pages of cattle prices on the desk in the corner.

'We've escaped lightly, you know,' said Sara, nodding at Maureen and tilting her head, with a smile, towards her husband. The two women had been having a hard time with him. 'Henry tells me we're thirty-two pockets up on last year so far already.'

'How many did we bring in last year? Three hundred?'

'Two-six-six.'

'So with any luck they might bring down the price of the ruddy beer so we can afford to drink the ruddy stuff.'

'Or put some more ruddy hops into the ruddy beer, more to the point,' said Sara, returning to her figures.

As well as being in considerable pain, Tony was in an uncomfortable mood, at once feeling sorry for himself, and boiling with frustration. He'd spent an irascible ten days in hospital, and now the doctors had bound up his chest, buried his foot in plaster, and told him he must use his crutches for at least another six weeks.

Tony had been admiring a yearling bull in the Newbury show ring when the animal had been distracted by a young woman and a baby in a pram close behind. It had suddenly shot off at high speed, knocking a woman right off her chair, narrowly missing Sara and sending Tony into a sensational backward somersault.

'People think a ruddy great bull is like a dog or a cat on the end of a lead, you can stroke it, or pet it, or do what you like with it. Like hell you can! One pat in the wrong place and I end up doing one hell of a Fosbury Flop!'

Now even breathing was painful, and coughing or laughing was quite out of the question. Far from being sympathetic, Sara had started to giggle when he'd got stuck in the bath last night, unable to reach the plug, his plastered foot wrapped in a plastic bag and dangling over the side, unable to twist back to turn off the taps, and he'd gone through purgatory trying not to laugh, which of course had made her giggle even more. 'You'd never had made a ruddy nurse, Florence Nightingale!' he'd yelled. Even the memory of it was agony.

'You should have seen his face when the specialist said six more weeks,' Sara said to Maureen. 'He was like a little boy who'd had something taken away from him. I really thought he was going to burst into tears, poor thing. Now he's like a bear with a sore head.'

It could have been worse; with the harvest nearly in, the ploughing and drilling could look after itself. The shooting was well booked, the pheasant chicks had had a good hatching season with not a sign of wet feet, and there were plenty of partridges about. Now it was a case of hoping for a good fall of winter snow to kill the spiders and any other objectionable bugs, and to sit it out until February, when they'd start again down in the hop-gardens, repairing, wireworking, planting.

Besides, there was Chris; his half-sisters Pom and Sally were now living in London, but Chris was firmly established in his little cottage beside Maureen on the other side of Hole Lane, ever eager to take over more responsibility on the farm, growing in confidence by the day. Over the years, they had tried to avoid putting pressure on him, but after agricultural college at Cirencester and three months working on a farm in Chile, Tony and Sara were delighted to hear that all he'd wanted to do was to return to Glade Farm, and in so doing continue the dynasty.

'Of course we're pleased,' Tony said. 'He wants to do it, so good luck to him. As for the dynasty, well, you never know, Chris might get married and have two wives – '

'What do you mean, have two wives?' demanded Sara.

'Sorry, I mean, two daughters – '

'What are you suggesting, Tony, he's going to commit bigamy, for God's sake?'

'Well, you never know your luck!'

At Bentley, the main line is reduced to a single track for its final two miles' run down to Alton, so only one platform is ever in use; quite why the Victorian designer built a footbridge and a southern platform, no one can be sure, for there's no reason to cross. The place is doted over by John, the station porter, who lovingly sweeps and scrubs and paints in the long periods between trains, and whose geraniums are regarded as second to none.

The journey down from London is only just over an hour, passing through Woking, Aldershot and Farnham, so it was with no surprise, although much muttering about 'progress', that the villagers watched the huge new 'young executive' estate of Eggars Field spring up on land between the school and the old Babs Field council houses, and gradually fill with commuters.

'They're young marrieds, no children, both work, so first thing in the morning they're out, back last thing in the evening, don't have anything to do with the rest

Bentley Station

of us,' said Sara. 'Tony was born and bred in the village, and there was a time not so long ago when he knew every single person living here. Not any more though.'

Suddenly there was the sound of gently hissing brakes, followed by the slam of half a dozen carriage doors which went off in the still afternoon air like gunshots.

'Hello, Maureen?'

The girl was smiling at her, a young, glamorous, London face, thought Maureen.

'I'm Emma, from *Woman's Own.*'

Maureen drove her back up Hole Lane, Emma keeping up an unending string of questions as they drove through the village, unable to hide entirely the faint note of incredulity that anyone could conceivably choose to live quite so far away from London.

'So tell me all about it,' Emma said later, sipping her tea and switching on the small tape-recorder she'd placed on the arm of the chair. In the kitchen,

Maureen's dog kept barking, and the budgie was having a field day. 'When did you first know something was wrong?'

'We didn't know anything was wrong until the moment Catherine was born,' said Maureen, after taking a deep breath. She tried to avoid looking at the tape recorder. 'The scans showed nothing, you see. She was born two months prematurely, and she came first, followed by her bowel and intestine, which had grown outside the body. They told me immediately. The second she was born she was taken into a corner, and there was a lot of whispering. The two midwives were arguing about whether I should hold her – one said yes, the other said no. I did eventually get to hold her, for about ten seconds, and they whisked her away, and came back with a photo of her.'

'So that's all you had, just a picture?'

Maureen nodded. 'I held that photo very tight. Then they said they wanted a name, because there would be a priest ready to baptise her – we'd only thought of boy's names, so she's called by my second name. Neil, my husband, said "Why do they want to christen her?" and I said, "Because she might die, of course," and this midwife said, "I don't want to hear you talk like that again!"

'We'd been taken to Great Ormond Street, where they operated, but her little body simply wasn't big enough to hold all her insides, so they put everything in bag above her bed, like a drip, and every day they lowered the clip, feeding it gradually back inside her day by day, as she grew bigger.'

'How much did she weigh?'

'She started at three pounds fourteen, but after the second operation she dropped to under two pounds. She didn't eat for four months. Doll's clothes were too big for her. If she was a boy, they said, she would have undoubtedly have died. Boys aren't as strong as girls, but she's a fighter. And now you'd never know,' she added, giving Emma a photograph from the mantelpiece of a blonde, smiling, toothy eleven-year old girl. 'She'll be home from school soon.'

'And now all she wants is a tummy-button?'

'That's right.'

'What an incredible story,' said Emma.

The Reverend Rogers decided it was high time to pay a visit to Glade Farm. He had been planning to drop in for weeks, but he could never be certain of finding the Holmes at home, being farming folk, and not exactly frequent attenders at St Mary's.

With Tony now laid up, though, he knew he'd be sure of finding someone there, so after easing his ample frame into his rather small car, he set off from the vicarage at Binsted, down past the Old Mill at Isington, where old Field Marshal Montgomery had lived for so many years, left by the station, along the lane winding through the meadows of the Wey and adjacent fields, which soon, he'd heard, were going to be ripped up for the bypass, over Anstey Bridge, across that devilish main road and eventually into Hole Lane.

A difficult task lay ahead of him at Glade Farm, particularly since his call was unrequested, but then, he told himself, the life of a village priest is never short of difficult tasks. Nevertheless, it was with a slightly heavy heart that he drove up and over the hill above Bury Court, leaving the valley behind, to see in front of him the stark outline of Glade House, set against another grey, forbidding sky.

He revved up the steep drive and parked in front of the house. Dogs barked. He knocked, twice. Even in the gloom he could see right across the valley, to the great forest opposite, and the site of the old semaphore tower, one of a line of towers along which even in Napoleonic times a message could be sent from Portsmouth to Whitehall in less than four minutes.

No-one was at home, not even Tony.

But then it wasn't Tony he'd come to see.

'Five-one-four-two-three!' said Henry Thompson, swinging both his beefy arms way above his head, pausing for a moment, then, with perfect timing, loading his considerable weight on to the rope for the downpull. Clearly, he'd done this before.

'One-five-two-four-three!'

Henry is a man of few words, like many a cattleman. After harvest, he's in charge of drying out the hops, but his main job is looking after Sara's herd of little black Dexter cattle. And now here he was, having taken over from old Walter as Captain of the Bells, giving Monday evening instruction in the ancient belltower of St Mary's.

Beside him was the new boy, a rather apprehensive Brian Wilkins, whom Henry had press-ganged into service one evening in the hop-shed when he thought Brian had had a particularly good day.

'If you can't get anyone else, Henry, I'll have a go,' Brian had said, on the spur of the moment. 'The Church and bell-ringing is part of village life, isn't it Henry, everyone expects to hear the bells, somebody's got to do it.' And with that, Brian had forgotten all about it.

Now he had been forced to forfeit an evening with the boys at the Prince of Wales, and was finding it hard going, despite the board Henry had set up on an easel opposite them both, with the sequences marked out in huge numbers.

'C'mon Brian, keep up. Five-one-four-two-three!'

Pulling beside Brian was Miss Margaret Evans, and beside her, old Walter, who had offered to help to teach Brian. Walter had pulled at Bentley for no less than forty-eight years, and had founded a bell-ringing dynasty. Beside Walter was his son, Richard, and beside him, on the treble, Walter's grandson, young Ross.

'It's been in the family, see. Grandad got Dad started on the treble when he was eleven, and then when I was eleven they put me on the treble.'

'When's your first Sunday morning pull, Brian?' asked Walter.

'My debut, you mean?' said Brian grandly. 'Sunday week.'

'We've a bit of work to do before then,' said Walter. 'For a start, you're trying to grab it when it comes level with your nose. That won't do, you musn't do that, let your hands go with it.

'Long years ago 'twas now, when Mr Inwood was the sexton here, he'd just been sent off to the First World War, so when there was a funeral his wife thought she'd have a go on the tenor. She grabbed hold of the rope, Brian, but she didn't let it go, so it came down, and then it took her up again.'

'Must be sixty foot up there.'

'She hung right on, so it took her up nearly to the ceiling.'

'You don't want to do that Sunday week,' said Henry, quietly.

FIVE

Every morning and every evening of the year, Sara would drive down the hill from Glade Farm to the fields and cattle-sheds at Bury Court, where she kept her beloved Belties and Dexters. With autumn, after calving comes the ear-tagging, and the agonising decisions over which bull-calves might bring home trophies from the show ring, and should therefore not be castrated, and which should be steered, destined for an unspectacular future in the deep freeze.

It was a decision she liked to share with her cattlemen. Bob Bates was in charge of the Belties and Henry Thompson of the curious little half-sized black Dexters for which she held a special affection. Together they would pace up and down endlessly, pontificating on confirmation, length of body, quality of back-end, and presence. Sometimes they would argue for hours over whether the bull looked too ugly, or too feminine, and the poor beast would listen silently to first one, then the other, and no doubt ponder the chances of surviving through to the end of next week, as God had intended, with all its organs intact.

'We've made some whopping great mistakes, and cut them when we jolly well shouldn't have, and later bitterly regretted it, haven't we Henry?'

'We live by our mistakes, don't we, Mrs Holmes.'

It was this daily proximity to the cattle Sara loved so much that led doctors to believe that when she had suddenly fallen ill more than a year ago, she was the victim of some rare cattle-borne disease. For a woman still in her forties, so full of energy and laughter, the discovery of an abscess in the chest came as an over-whelming blow.

'Most extraordinary, it appeared overnight, a freakish thing. It hadn't grown from a small lump: suddenly one morning, there it was.

'My first thought was, cancer! but they said no, because I was working with cattle all the time, and I had every symptom of anthrax, I was even running a raging temperature. Now, there aren't many doctors in Hampshire who've ever seen a case of anthrax, so they all got frightfully excited and started jumping up and down, admitted me that weekend, took a whole series of tests, and operated the following day.

'After they'd operated, the surgeon came and told me that he'd had a jolly good poke around, and decided that it wasn't anthrax, but some other, even rarer, bovine infection of the blood, and they got even more excited. I stayed in hospital for five days. On the fifth day they announced that during the op. they'd taken some histology samples, the results of which had just come through: I had, after all, got cancer.

'My first reaction was sheer rage. Why should it be me? What had I done to deserve it? And there is this terrible feeling that cancer is a death sentence, which is pretty stupid when you think there are thousands of people walking around who've been cured. Why shouldn't I survive? Then I got very melodramatic. Will I ever see my daughters married? Will I ever see my grandchildren?

'I'm very honest with people. I do tell them I've got cancer, and most of them are frankly terrified. They think it's contagious. It's rather like having a death in the family, they don't want to look you straight in the eyes in case you burst into tears or have a fit of the screaming heebie-jeebies. I remember someone telling me when my first husband died, don't be worried when you see someone you know crossing the street, because they're embarrassed, they're at a loss. It's very British, never wanting to show your emotions, stiff upper lip.'

So began a long and heroic battle; first there were daily trips down to Southampton for what Sara called her 'blastings', the sessions under the radiotherapy machine. Then a lymph gland was removed, and later she had a mastectomy.

'They even told me not to go to the Royal Show this year, but I said, to hell with you, I'm going anyway! So I had three courses of radiotherapy before the Show, then I came back and finished the course. I don't think they meet many people who are bloody-minded enough to tell them that they want to enjoy themselves, as well as having treatment. You might get run over by a bus tomorrow. To my mind, life is for living, not for moping about.'

Now had come news that the treatment had failed. The cancer had reappeared, this time in the pelvic bone, and for the next week she'd be returning to Southampton every day for another series of blastings.

Her appointments were mid-day, so she would still be able to join Bob and Henry in the cattle-sheds, mornings and evenings.

'It's the little things which are so ruddy annoying. They've marked me with some kind of pencil so the radiographer knows precisely where to direct the beam, so I'm not allowed a bath all week in case the mark comes off. And if you can't have something, you want it even more. For someone like me, not being allowed to bath is absolute purgatory.

'But I have got it, and I think the more people know about those who've got cancer, the less frightening it is. They can look at me, and say, she survived for a year, she's done all the things she's wanted to do. If I get it, why can't I be like Sara?'

'I'm still having my evening slug of Scotch, though; they've not forbidden me that because I've not told them about it, and I have no intention of doing so, too damn right!'

These where not happy days for Henry Thompson. After saying goodnight to Mrs Holmes and putting the Dexters to bed, he set off wearily through the long evening shadows, down the track between the fields that led from the back of Bury Court to the church, and on down to the Babs Field council estate.

His niece, Denise, was expecting him.

'Sorry about Kevin's job,' he said, after she'd given him a cup of tea.

'We couldn't believe it. Kevin just came in from work, and said that as of this afternoon, Crosby Doors of Farnham no longer exists. The entire workforce has been made redundant.'

'After all those promises about promotion.'

'Nobody on the shopfloor had a clue. Kevin's only been there twelve years, but some of them have worked for Crosby's thirty or forty years.'

'Nobody wants doors in a recession.'

'The factory's on a prime residential site.'

Kevin and Denise had an eleven-year-old daughter and five-year-old twins, a boy and a girl. Over the last few years they had worked ceaselessly to make something of their council house: they had decorated, carpeted, fitted out the kitchen, were now just about to make a start on the lounge they had been stripping out for weeks, and all in anticipation of one day being able to buy the house, as soon as Kevin's promotion had come through.

Now all they had to rely on were Denise's earnings as a child-minder. That wouldn't pull in much. She was paid just over one pound an hour, and out of that she had to provide them with lunch. Kevin had been telling her for years she was daft to do it for so little, but she worried about the children, and how much they depended on her. The parents of one of the two five-year-olds she cared for had even asked Kevin and Denise if they'd take her on holiday with them. 'She'd probably enjoy it more with your family,' they'd said to Denise. 'She'd be bored with us.' Kevin had said no, not on your nelly.

'It would be heartbreaking if we have to move because of Kevin's job,' said Denise. 'Apart from the house, I've all my family here. And I want all my children to go to school here, I want them to grow up here.'

'Quite right,' said Henry.

'Bill Rogers called in the other day,' said Sara, through the window of the Range Rover.

'Did he?' said Tony, astonished. 'What did he want?'

'Asked if I'd mind if they prayed for my health in the church. Bit ominous, I thought, but I told him I didn't mind, it couldn't do any harm. Toodle-oo!'

'Got enough petrol?'

'Half a tank.'

'Plenty.'

By now, the three-quarter-hour journey from Bentley down to Southampton, through Alton, Bishop's Waltham and the autumnal delights of the Meon Valley, had become irritatingly familiar. Although the radiography left Sara with no unpleasant side-effects, she recognised the familiar feeling of unease as she drew up outside the hospital and tried to find somewhere to park. The place was always overflowing with cars.

'It's so terribly depressing, going into the unit. It's a very sixties building, all lino and glass everywhere reflecting the bands of strip-lighting. You're at a low anyway when you come in here, you really want something which is going to lift your spirits. There are no flowers, no cheerful colours, nothing remotely optimistic, just rows of silent people, waiting, waiting, waiting.'

'Mrs Holmes, I'm here to see Dr Ryall,' she said to the receptionist.

'Would you mind waiting?'

The radiotherapy machines at the Royal Southampton Hospital provide treatment for people from a huge area of southern England – from Hampshire, Wiltshire, Dorset, Isle of Wight, even the Channel Islands. The machines start at eight in the morning, and don't stop until six.

Sara sat and nodded, smiling, to a few familiar faces. Some of them smiled back. 'Bit like a production line. All that's missing is the smell of cabbage. Staff are wonderful, though. Glad to see the clocks are working properly. At the beginning of the year, when I first came, every single clock said a completely different time. You never really knew how late or early you were. Very clever.'

A young woman opposite, her arm around a grey-faced husband, forced a laugh.

'How is Bill?' asked Sara, and a moment of fear crossed the face of the woman.

'Not much different.'

'Did they have to give you more purple yesterday?'

The man nodded.

'Bad luck!'

The first time Sara had had the treatment, she had been very frightened.

'It's such an unknown quantity: you're left in this dark room on your own, there's a beam, and you're mind works overtime. But really, there's nothing to worry about. There's nothing to it.'

The treatment took less than two minutes, and was painless. Sara lay on the bed. The radiographer, after making sure the beam was directed exactly onto the pencil mark on her skin, withdrew. There was a short, high-pitched whine from the machine, and it was all over.

'Till tomorrow, then.'

''Bye, Mrs Holmes.'

In the bell tower of the church the ringers were arriving, one by one.

'Mornin', Walter. Mornin', Richard, Ross.'

'Mornin', Brian,' said three generations of Sher-fields in unison.

'Mornin', Henry.'

'Mornin', Brian.'

'Mornin', Miss Evans.'

'Good morning, Brian.'

This was the moment the village had been waiting for. Brian stood in front of his rope, very smartly dressed, but strangely pale and fidgety.

'He's all right,' said Walter. 'You'll be ringing well this morning, won't you Brian?'

'I'll do me best,' said Brian, with a nervous giggle.

'You only just got up?' asked Henry.

'I've been up since the crack of dawn this morning, but I still only just managed to get ready in time. It's the wind that's ruined me hairstyle – well, what hair I've got left, anyway.'

'You nervous?'

'Me throat's gone dry, and I'm sweating.'

'He'll be all right,' said Walter again.

'Look two!' piped up young Ross. 'Two's going . . . she's gone!'

Suddenly the old timbers of the bell-tower, already weakened by the ravages of the death-watch beetle, began vibrating to the deafening broadside of the first peal.

'Well done Brian,' thought the Revd Rogers, as he revved up, shot over the crossroads, and raced up Hole Lane, leaving a cloud of dust behind him. He'd been listening to the Bentley bells since hurrying out after morning service at Binsted Church, four miles away on the other side of the parish. Every Sunday it was a dash from one church to the other.

Weaving in and out of the small groups of church-goers, narrowly missing a small boy on a bicycle, he pulled up outside the lych-gate with minutes to spare.

'Morning, General.'

'Morning, Rogers.'

A breathless Mrs Bonner met him at the door.

'We're nearly out of wafers, Mr Rogers.'

'There should be five hundred wafers somewhere, but I've got plenty at home, so there should be no problem. I bought two boxes last time, one as a reserve – I wonder where the other one is?'

'You don't think anyone would have eaten them, do you?'

He struggled into his cassock, and nodded at Mr Snooke, the organist.

'Six and out!' said Henry. Through the little window at the end of the nave he'd caught sight of the first of the choir moving forward to begin the service.

Walter looked at this protégé with obvious pride. For Brian, the morning had been a triumph.

'Once I got going I was fine,' he said, beaming. 'I nearly sent Henry up to the belfry a couple of times, 'cos I was throwing me arms out when I was pulling down, and you start to lose control of the rope, don't you – '

'Just as I'd warned – ' said Walter.

'But I didn't let go, Walter, not once!'

'I think he's done marvellous,' said Walter, as the others patted Brian on the back. 'Couldn't have done better myself.'

Outside the great white front door of Jenkyn Place, Patricia Coke could see a tall, broad-shouldered, strong-featured woman in her thirties, with very long, striking blonde hair which she constantly flicked back over the collar of her raincoat. In fact, the visitor was rather glamorous, not at all what Mrs Coke had been expecting.

'How very nice to see you,' she said, as the house-keeper swung open the door.

'Marian Dampier-Jeans, how do you do?'

'Very unusual name.'

'I'm Danish, you see.'

They stood in the hall, each intrigued by the other.

'You're a medium?'

'A spiritualist medium.'

'You look terribly normal, if you don't mind me saying so.'

'I am terribly normal.'

'I really don't know what I expected.'

The reason Marian had come down to Bentley

from her home in London was that for a number of
years Mrs Coke had believed that Jenkyn Place was
haunted. Indeed, there was one room in the house
which ever since they had moved in fifty years ago
made Mrs Coke feel distinctly uneasy whenever she
entered it. Before buying the house, they were shown
around it by old Miss Eggar, who was one of the last of
the family which had lived in the house for generations
until 1905. Even she had said there was something
strange about the room, although despite their questions the old lady had steadfastly refused to discuss it.

'What do you want to do? Are you a person who
likes to go straight to the ghost, or what?'

'I've never been here before, I've never met you
before, I don't know anything about any hauntings
here, so it's very nice just to walk about. If you could
show me from room to room, and let's see if we can find
the cold spot.'

So Mrs Coke led her guest from the hall, with its
huge, circular balustrade above, and through to the
reception rooms. As they walked, they chatted away
like old friends.

'When did you first realise you had psychic
powers?'

'I used to walk over to the local graveyard, and sit on
top of the stones, and talk to the people who the vicar had
just buried. He used to come up to me and say, OK
Marian, what are you doing now, and I'd say, I'm chatting
to the people you've just buried, and I could describe them
to him, and tell him their names, even though I was only
five or six. I made his hair stand on end.'

'Really?' said Mrs Coke. 'Yes, this small room,
which we use as a study, used to be the dining-room,
part of the old house facing east. Come on through.'

'It's lovely.'

'The Sandersons lived here for a short time – the White Star Line people. One night when they were having dinner in this very room, a telegram arrived saying that the *Titanic* had gone down. It had an awful effect on Mr Sanderson, as you can imagine. Apparently he never spoke again.'

Up at the other big house in the village, Marsh House, to the east, there were signs of great activity on the long, winding drive which snakes elegantly through the huge sweep of parkland to the front.

Marsh House looks as though it could have been the perfect setting for a Jane Austen novel, which indeed it could easily have been, since the novelist herself lived the last few years of her life a few miles away down the Alton road, at Chawton. Built as a modest country house in the late eighteenth century, Marsh House was extended in 1848, and two imposing wings were added in 1909. It is now the home of Colonel Harrap, and today he was busying about, carrying out last minute preparations in his role as host to the first hunt of the season.

When Lord Stawell owned Marsh House in the eighteenth century, he kept a pack of 'Staunch Hounds' kennelled in the Alice Holt forest opposite, but since 1825 this has been part of the territory of the Hampshire Hunt, always known as the 'H.H.' Already a row of horseboxes was lining the grass beside the drive, and a large van-load of glum-looking policemen, now almost as much a part of the tradition as the hounds themselves, was parked out of sight by the

greenhouses at the back of the house, in anticipation of the usual pack of hunt saboteurs.

The Colonel is a rather distinguished-looking, whiskery-haired old gentleman who at one time was chairman of the parish council, many years before Tony Holmes took over. He had instructed Ron, the part-time gardener, to position a large trestle-table on the gravel terrace outside the front door, and now Maxine was bringing out a huge tray loaded with over fifty glasses of port for the hunters.

'We used to give 'em cherry brandy, but it got a bit expensive,' said the Colonel. 'Have a glass, my dear.'

'We used to call it "Jumping Powder", to give them Dutch courage for the ride,' said Mrs Harrap, following her husband's example. 'We don't ride now, too old, I'm afraid.'

'In the old days when there were two divisions and the cavalry brigade stationed over at Aldershot, we'd get hundreds of officers over here for the hunt, an

Marsh House,
where the 'H.H.'
meets

enormous field. Today, maybe we'll get fifty or sixty
riders. It's a Friday, you see.'

This is a great village occasion, when families walk
up to see the hounds set off, and then follow on foot as
far as they can.

'They'll first draw the woods behind the house,
but what with the main road in front and the people at
Northfoot next door, who won't have us because they
breed ponies, there are only two directions to get the
foxes a-foot. Pity, really. Not like it used to be.'

In the scullery, Kathleen and her niece Maxine
were busy making up rows of Gentleman's Relish
sandwiches. Kathleen had been born on the farm after
her father, a carter, came to work for the Harraps in the
First World War. Kathleen does the upstairs of Marsh
House, whilst Maxine does downstairs. 'And if they
have a dinner-party, I do my favourite job. I wait at
table,' said Kathleen.

'Diamonds or fingers, Mrs 'arrap?'

'Oh, diamonds, I think, Kathleen. Aren't they easier to eat on horseback? And don't forget to remove the crusts.'

Out front, the Colonel was having a natter with one of his oldest friends, Tony Holmes. Neither Tony nor Sara hunted, but both enjoyed the company of the Harraps, and this was an occasion not to be missed.

'Lovely day again, Mike,' said Tony, leaning on his crutches.

'Always wet at the end of October, but do you know it's always fine for the meet here at Marsh House,' said the Colonel. 'I've got photographs going back to the end of the last century, and it's always dry and sunny. Quite extraordinary. We had one wet meet just after the War, but that's because the Master got the date wrong, and came the second Saturday of November, instead of the first. What have you got on your foot, Tony?'

Tony was wearing one of a pair of huge, multi-coloured trainers on his injured foot, the largest he'd been able to find in the shops.

'The physio said I should put on these ruddy things, to support the ankle. Forty-nine quid the pair! And I only need one of them!'

'How are you managing?'

'Going round the bend, Mike, can't do a ruddy thing. If it wasn't for the automatic, I'd be stuck at home all day, too. Sara's down at Southampton every day this week for her latest set of blastings.'

'Of course.'

The two men were silent for a minute, watching the horses being saddled up.

'Not many Antis about, Mike.'

'I think it's because the hunt's on a Friday this year, not a Saturday, so perhaps they can't get time off.

We saw somebody wandering about suspiciously last night. Whether or not they were spying out the lie of the land I don't know. The police look a bit disappointed. Have a glass of port, Tony.'

'Cheers, God bless!' said Tony, downing the port. 'Roll on next year. Got to be better than this.'

Despite the bravado, Tony's thoughts were never far away from Sara, and her ever-present ordeal.

'It's difficult to talk about it, particularly to Sara direct. Pom and Sally have been very good about it, very business-like, saying, come on Mummy, you can't do this, you must do that, and young Fogs has been remarkable, especially since she was there within five minutes of Sara being told initially she had cancer. A couple of her friends at school have parents who've had cancer and survived, so that's something good.

'But Sara has accepted that the cancer is there, and she's not going to give in, she's going to fight it. She's not going to sit down, and do nothing, and knit or something – she can't knit anyway – she'll fight it, she's not the giving-in sort, I can tell you that.

'Roll on next year, I say, and forget this one. Stuff it!'

'This is the library, which was added on much later,' said Mrs Coke, leading her guest into the next room. 'All that area was originally farm sheds, and this I suppose was the living-room of the old house. Gerald had it converted to take all his books and manuscripts.'

'What a beautiful room,' said Marian.

'Can I tell you something strange about it?'

'Of course, that's why I'm here.'

'An old friend of ours, John Christie, of Glynde-bourne fame, was staying here, and one day after dinner he was sitting on that chair there, and I was here, playing with a child. Suddenly he said, Tricia, who's that woman over there? and described our little Victorian housekeeper, standing just over there, at the bottom of the stairs. I've never seen her myself, but at least two of our old friends, both dead now, have seen her on different occasions, and both described her in exactly the same way: a small woman, obviously a servant, going up or down the stairs. That's just what John saw, that night. He was really rattled, poor man. He rushed to telephone his son, left next day, and never returned.'

'I think that's very sad,' said Marian. 'His faith could have been shattered, you see, where he didn't have any belief in the spirit world, didn't believe in anything like that.'

'I think he thought it was a knock on the door, that it was a message to him that he didn't have long himself. And he died shortly afterwards.'

Marian moved about the room, constantly looking about her, her fingers gently moving through the air.

'I'm positive you don't really want to get rid of her, this little housekeeper,' Marian said at length.

'No, she's nice.'

'She's part of the furniture, isn't she? She's probably looking after the place, making sure everyone who comes in here is OK.'

'What a nice idea. You're very encouraging.'

'There aren't any bad vibrations here in this room, nor the others I've been into on the ground floor. It's all very calm, and there are visits here by very many spirits, not just the housekeeper. I can feel it, look, my hands can't keep still. This is a lovely room.'

'We felt that about the house as a whole, when we first came here,' said Mrs Coke. 'Except for one room, that is. I'm terribly un-ghostly, you might say, but there's one room I won't go into, particularly after dark. I'm not going to tell you which one. See if you can find out.'

Mrs Coke gestured Marian forward, and together the two women began walking slowly up the old, wooden staircase.

=== SEVEN ===

The flames took hold faster than anyone had thought, least of all Kevin, who retreated backwards as fast as he could go on all-fours, back through the tunnel he had carefully created when they had began to build the fire three weeks before.

Once safely out he stood catching his breath as the growing orange glow moved swiftly up and outwards, so that at last the crowd could start to make out the huge silhouette of the bonfire against the darkness. Last year the fire hadn't burnt out until the early morning; now, after the summer's drought, it could all be over in an hour or so.

Over the years it had become Kevin's job to light the school Guy Fawkes' Night bonfire on the green by the cricket pitch, with the grass still worn from the summer fête and flower show, and he took a certain pride in it; but this year the jollity which usually surrounded the occasion was proving difficult to summon up.

It looked, after all, as though he and Denise and the family would have to move away from the village.

He had applied for any number of jobs, but there had been no calls for interview, and the only firm offer had come from the parent company to Crosby's, who wanted him to move to their head office a hundred miles away in Swindon. Denise had been very upset, although she had not let anyone know it.

'See the twin guys, right at the top?' Kevin had spent the day making a pair of identical guys for the twins. 'It's an excuse for the dads to have a good time. None of the guys are ever made by the children, are they? Want a sparkler, Lee?'

There seemed no alternative to the Swindon move, even though it would nearly break them financially, despite a small increase in Kevin's wages. The problem was that they'd have no choice but to take out a mortgage to buy a house, since in that part of Wiltshire there is a seven-year waiting list for council houses. A mortgage, even a small one, would cost them three times what they now paid in rent.

They stood and watched the brilliant orange and silver explosions in the night sky, a strangely hypnotic sight. Illuminated dramatically from above, the familiar buildings of the village centre – the Victorian school, the cricket pavilion, Fox Hall beside the old pond where once had stood the stocks, whipping post and ducking stool, the Old Rectory on the other side of the main road where Jane Austen's brother Henry had lived – all were casting weird, monstrous shadows. Kevin and the family watched, not saying, but only too aware, that this was probably the last firework display they'd see in Bentley, and that next year someone else would have to be found to light the bonfire.

On the other side of the field, Tony was chatting to Jim Harden, Glade Farm's maintenance man, who lived in one of Tony's cottages down by the banks of the Wey.

'Did you see those wretched mink hounds down by the river the other day, Jim?' said Tony. It was unusual to see him at a social event alone, but Sara had not been feeling well enough to join him.

'Heard about 'em, Mr Holmes, from the folk living near the station.'

'I could have heard them from Glade House. Hell of a thing. Apparently the fishing society had asked them to come up from Devon, and get rid of the mink, but I haven't seen a mink for years, have you?'

'Heard of one down by the bridge a bit back.'

'Never asked me about it. Straight over my land. Some of those people have got ducks on the water – they went, of course, and haven't been back. Hounds went charging through my cattle. We've got thirty heifers in calf down there, haven't we Jim? They went berserk. I got on the blower to the fishing society, I said this isn't on, you've got to ask people before you go rampaging onto their land. There were forty people or so there, you know. I'm afraid I rather fell out with them.'

'I'm not surprised, Mr Holmes.'

'How's your daughter, Jim?'

'Cherie? Oh, not so bad. We're waiting for some news from America.'

Cherie Harden was another young girl who had become well-known locally through an accident of fate. As a young child, she was diagnosed as suffering an oversized spleen, but the doctors had said she would be able to lead a normal life, and so she did, at least to start with. It was only after she left Bentley Primary School and had moved on to Eggar's at Alton, that her parents grew concerned; she was constantly falling over and coming home with unexplained bruises. Eventually, after endless tests, a neurologist told Jim that his daughter was one of only a hundred known sufferers worldwide of a degenerative illness of the liver called Niemann-Pick's disease. This leads to an accumulation of cholesterol deposits in the liver and the brain, leaving the victim with clumsy movements and slurred speech. No treatment had yet been found.

'What's the news from America?' asked Tony.

'I'll let you know if it comes to anything, Mr Holmes.'

'Anything I can do to help, I will.'

Later, after the bonfire party was over, Kevin and Denise took the children home to bed, and when Denise's mother had arrived to babysit for them, they drove into Farnham for the last ever disco at the Crosby's Social Club.

Usually the Crosby discos were hilarious; but tonight, they all agreed, turned out to be a rather damp affair.

Mrs Coke and Marian were slowly working their way around every room in Jenkyn Place. They had now reached the last bedroom on the first floor, and still not an inkling of a cold spot, despite all the creaking floor boards.

'This was originally two rooms, children's rooms, when we first came here,' said Mrs Coke. 'It's such a long time ago now, I can scarcely remember the details. All right in here?'

'Lovely, I love the view.' Outside, they could just make out the church tower, beyond the fields, and the little roof of John O'Pease Cottage.

Mrs Coke led Marian up another set of wooden stairs, and into the attic of the old house.

'This is also a nice room, can you feel it? It's got a warm atmosphere, a cosy feel, hasn't it?' said Marian.

'When I had babies, I always used to move into this room for the first few weeks, it's so cosy,' replied Mrs Coke.

'Beautifully decorated, beautiful furniture.'

The next room, however, drew a very different response. Like many of the other rooms on this floor, the old roof beams which framed either side of the dormer windows were exposed, but there were also exposed upright beams half-way along each wall, which suggested that this, too, had had a dividing wall removed. There was little furniture.

Marian stopped dead, and carefully looked around her.

'Now this room,' she said, 'is not like the others.'

Mrs Coke couldn't take her eyes off Marian's face. 'No?'

'This room has a colder atmosphere.'

She walked slowly from the doorway, down through the room, towards the window.

'Just feel it down here. Even when you come through the door, its there, but down this end it's colder. Not cold because there's no fire. Just cold.'

'There were two rooms, again,' said Mrs Coke, talking very quickly now. 'This was the room we altered when we moved in, and old Miss Eggar said, thank heavens you've done that, but she never said why.'

'It's this end, definitely this end,' Marian was saying. 'I can feel it. You don't come in here?'

'Not unless I have to, and certainly never after dark.'

'Can you feel the cold?'

'Yes, I can. You're absolutely plum right, there were stories of people sleeping in here and being literally hurled out of bed. Bad stories.'

'That kind of thing happened to me as a child, but I'd be lifted carefully out of bed, and later lifted back in.' Marian was animated, almost excited. 'I'd love to sit on my own in this room for ten minutes, to find out what's going on.'

So without another word, Mrs Coke withdrew, leaving Marian alone.

After a few minutes of sitting quietly, with her eyes firmly closed, Marian stood up and began to pace across the far end of the room. Occasionally she would stop for a moment, close her eyes and then pop them suddenly open, and spin slowly in a clockwise direction. At one stage she held her arms around her shoulders, and swayed. Then she paced again.

Eventually she called out down the stairs, and Mrs Coke returned.

'The spirit made me go round in circles,' she said. 'Then I felt very unwell, and very dizzy. Then I felt I was swinging. What I have done now is energize the walls to give out a better feeling, a more loving feeling, and to send away anything that's there already. I have put in the light.'

'What do you think it was?'

'It was a build-up of sorrow, of sadness. At one point I wanted to cry, I could feel the tears welling up . . . a lot of unhappiness, unhappy memories. Somebody was locked in this room, somebody was trapped in here. There was a lot of cruelty, of mental cruelty. Someone was being treated very badly, almost tortured, and that has left a scar on the room. Now it is a little lighter. Do you feel it?

75

'Yes, I do,' said Mrs Coke without hesitation. 'I feel it's . . . well, lighter is the only word for it.'

'It's like feeling, oh good, that's a relief?'

'Yes. Something has happened here. And now it feels different, better.'

Later, Mrs Coke took Marian downstairs for a glass of sherry, and after chatting pleasantly for a few minutes, the medium put on her raincoat and set off back to London.

'I'll let you know after the winter if that room still feels the same!' said Mrs Coke, as Marian's car pulled away. But she didn't; she still hasn't summoned courage enough to return to the room and its mysterious chill.

D own at Babs Field, Kevin spent a very long time indeed examining himself in the mirror. He wasn't used to wearing a suit, and looked slightly self-conscious in it, as though he was trying it out in the shop and couldn't quite make up his mind. His favourite red and blue striped tie felt uncomfortably tight around the throat.

'You'll be fine, you look great, just be yourself,' Denise reassured him. At last, Kevin had had some luck. Just as they had resigned themselves to leaving the village, a company a few miles away on the outskirts of Farnham, with a vacancy in quality control, had approached him. He hadn't even had to apply. It could mean they would be able to stay, and perhaps one day buy their house after all.

Kevin had never been through a formal interview before.

'I don't know what I'll be like when I go in. I'm a

bit shy anyway, but the thought of going into a room with a strange man, and talking about my life, and all of that, that's when I start losing words, going red, getting confused, and all the time he'll be staring at me.'

'It's the anticipation which is worrying you,' said Denise, putting an arm over his shoulder. 'It's the sitting waiting for it. But once you go in, I know you'll be all right, I know you will.'

It was half-term, so Louise, Michael and Lisa joined her on the doorstep to wave him off.

'Just a case of waiting now,' she said to them, as Kevin drove off to what could be the most important interview of his life.

EIGHT

Miss Hilda Evans lives with her sister Margaret in one of the oldest cottages in the village, tucked away behind the War Memorial Hall, from where the two sisters would regularly carry out rescue missions to victims of car accidents at the notorious junction of Hole Lane with the main road, bearing hot tea and home-made biscuits.

Hilda and Margaret are both retired school-mistresses, and since neither had married and so were unencumbered with time-consuming family problems, threw themselves into village life with an energy and an ardour that impressed even those who had known them for years.

Hilda is the younger, and more adventurous. Forty years ago she took a job as a teacher for a missionary society in what was then Nyasaland. For nine years she was based at a school on Likoma Island, in the middle of what is now called Lake Malawi, which then, as now, was full of crocodiles and rare tropical fish. 'I've even had fish named after me,' she would say, with some pride. 'Whilst I was on Likoma, a marine scientist discovered three previously unknown breeds of fish, and he called one of them Likomensis Evansii.' She'd always planned to return one day to Malawi, to find out what happened to some of her former pupils, and maybe catch a sight of Likomensis Evansii gurgling about happily in some rock pool on the beach.

On returning from Africa, Hilda joined Margaret at a private girls' school in Surrey, and later they both retired to Bentley, from where each summer Hilda launched expeditions to various mountain ranges around the world.

'So far I've done three trips to the Himalayas, and one to the Andes. Got togged up in all the right equipment, of course, boots, haversacks, the lot – you have to. We climbed up to sixteen thousand feet, you see. On that trip there were twelve of us, with thirty-one porters, six Sherpas and four cooks.'

'I normally stay at home and hold the fort,' said Margaret. 'But on Hilda's last trip to the Himalayas, I'd planned a separate holiday in the same area, but at slightly lower altitudes, with a friend. People around the village would say, how's Hilda getting on? is she all right? and I'd say she's out of contact for six weeks in the mountains, but I'm meeting her next Wednesday for lunch in Katmandu.'

At the centre of their great love of the village was the church. Margaret became a bell-ringer and volunteered as reserve organist to stand in for Mr Snooke, and she was always to be found at the Tuesday evening practice singing lustily with the choir.

Every five years St Mary's, most of which was built over eight hundred years ago, is inspected by a building surveyor, and the sisters had just seen a copy of his latest report. Death-watch beetle had been found in the tower timbers, and there was a suspicion that it might have chewed its way through the rest of the building, although until scaffolding could be erected they couldn't be sure.

'Giles reckons it's going to cost at least fifty thousand pounds,' said Margaret. 'How on earth are we going to raise that?'

U p at Glade Farm, Tony stood at the bottom of the stairs, brandishing a copy of the latest issue of *Woman's Own* magazine that they'd pushed under his nose in the Village Stores.

'Maureen! I've got something that might interest you here!'

His housekeeper came running down to the hall, and saw what he was holding.

'Oh, no.'

'Oh, yes!'

At first, she couldn't believe it; a double-page feature, under the banner headline I WAS BORN INSIDE OUT, NOW I'M GETTING A TUMMY-BUTTON, along with pictures of Catherine with her dog, the scars on her body, and shots of Catherine with Maureen, her father and sister.

'Listen to this,' said Maureen. ' "Little girls tend to dream of receiving mini-skirts, make-up sets and the latest Madonna record for their twelfth birthday, but young Catherine Parker has a very different dream indeed. 'All I've ever really wanted is a tummy-button,' she says quietly." ' Maureen laughed. 'She'll love that!'

'What else does it say?'

Maureen's eyes were racing down the page.

' "I blame myself," she explains. "I felt I must have done something wrong. The guilt was always there, even when the doctors told me it wasn't anything I'd done. The problem was a defect in the stomach wall – but it took a couple of months before I stopped blaming myself." It brings it all back, it makes me remember everything, it really does.'

'Well, you've done the right thing,' said Tony. 'These things shouldn't be bottled up. The more it comes out into the open, the easier it becomes for someone else in the same position. I think you'll help a lot of people.'

'Look at the end bit, here. "Catherine agrees. 'I can't believe Mum went through all that pain for me – but now I can definitely say I'm a mummy's girl!' " I can't wait to show her that, when she gets back from school!'

'Do you think she'll like it?'

'I think she'll get embarrassed, but I think it will help her understand exactly what happened to her, seeing it all in black and white like this. I don't think she's quite grasped it before.'

When Don, the postman, arrived, he asked if she could sign a copy of the magazine for him, and Maureen, blushing, said, yes, of course.

Elsewhere on the farm, life was quietening down for the winter. The winter wheat was drilled and the beans were in. Brian Wilkins was out in the hop-gardens with a team of men, repairing the wirework after the ravages of the summer.

Tony and Henry had been up the night before, watching over one of the pedigree Dexter herd, Prunella, who was calving. The little Dexters, which originated on the west coast of Ireland, only grow to three and a half feet. Sara had given each of her cows a name beginning with the letter P, after her own first married name, Pike. She had even called one after her daughter Pom.

'Your niece Denise moving out of the village, Henry?' Tony asked, as they watched Prunella gently lick the new calf in a corner of the field, separate from the rest of the herd.

'Kevin got the job, Mr Holmes.'

'He must be delighted.'

'He's not that confident a boy, he's done well. First job interview he's ever done.'

For Tony's maintenance man, Jim Harden, this was a time of year to catch up on all those jobs he had put off for months. During the harvest he worked from dawn to dusk with the welding equipment keeping the machinery going, and occasionally working manically through the night to try to breathe life into the old hop-picking machine when it broke down. Now, with the onset of winter, he was usually to be found down below the Dexters in his workshop by the great Hampshire corn barn at Bury Court, which until the war had housed the Victorian threshing machine. He was spending the time repairing bull pens and replacing broken prongs and shovel handles by the dozen, but at present, his mind was preoccupied with the future of his seventeen-year-old daughter, Cherie.

The doctors had told Jim that there was nothing more they could do for Cherie, and that Niemann-Pick's disease is progressively degenerative. Then, by chance, his doctor had discovered that an experimental treatment programme was being launched at the National Institute of Health in Maryland, USA. He had written to them, and they had invited Cherie to join twenty-three other sufferers from around the world in a series of bi-monthly experiments to establish an effective drug control of the disease.

'I thought I'd tell you the truth about what was happening, rather than you hear it on the grapevine,' he had said to Tony and Sara. 'Cherie's deteriorating, and this is our only chance.'

The National Institute had said that, once on American soil, all Cherie's expenses – her treatment, travel and accommodation – would be paid in full, but that they could not help finance the flights to Maryland.

Jim had contacted his ex-wife, Cherie's mother, and they had agreed to scrape up between them the seven hundred pounds that would be required to fly her and Cherie on the first round trip to America. For the year's remaining visits, a further five thousand pounds at least would have to be found, a figure Jim knew to be quite beyond him.

What, then, could he do? He wasn't the sort of man to go begging, that's for sure.

Tony was driving his daughter Fogs down to Alton to buy new clothes.

'Now you're to spend your own money this afternoon, Fogs, not Daddy's money. Remember your allowance, that magic allowance that never seems to get spent?' said Sara. 'And I want the money back for that suede coat . . . just a minor detail!'

'That's so unfair!'

'No it's not. You spent all your hop-picking money.'

'And I want to get the train set down later.'

'You're not to get the train set down. Granny Rowsell's coming this afternoon.'

'I am going to get the train set down.'

'You won't, because of all those spiders in the attic.'

'I'll get Granny Rowsell to get the train set down. 'Bye!'

''Bye!'

There was a pile of letters and other paperwork that Sara could not bring herself to attend to. She now found it difficult to walk, and reluctantly had agreed to leave the cattlework entirely to Bob and Henry. The latest set of blastings didn't seem to have worked.

'Cancer of the bone is one of the most painful forms of cancer. The pain can't escape, it's locked into the bone. The aim of the radiotherapy is to ossify the cancerous bone, and kill the pain in the process, but that hasn't happened, and I can't live for ever on painkillers. In the meantime, I'm having adriomycine injections twice a week, which make me feel a bit queasy, and chemotherapy pills every day, but that's all controllable. The trouble is that Tony hasn't been able to help me with the pain, and that's been difficult for him, not to be able to do anything.

'Another problem is that you can't plan. We had been hoping to go to Cornwall for ten days, we've had enough of doctors for the time being, but then you just can't do that. Also, its the unknown quantity of the thing. I want to know exactly what cancer looks like. What does it consist of? I can't visualise it. Nobody has time to tell you.'

Sara's family, along with Maureen, and Eileen Elpelt, who came up from Bury Court on Thursday mornings to help clean the brass, watched her battle, helplessly. At Glade House it was always openly discussed, although some of the villagers still found it difficult to approach Sara.

'Some of my friends have just been unable to cope with me, they're still terrified I'm going to burst into tears. Anyway, it's a damn good thing to cry, it lets the adrenalin flow away, it eases the pressure.

'I do get low at times, and I'm not particularly religious, although every time the cancer rears its ugly head again, I do wonder if there is a God. It's a cruel disease. But then I'm just as likely to go and have a large whisky instead.

'I've been lucky, too. This is an active farm, a business, and I'm still able to play an active role in it, which keeps my mind busy. Tony's around all the time, my family have been super. I think if I lived in a house on a big estate, and my husband went off at seven every morning and didn't get back until late, that would be a very different kettle of fish. Time is a dangerous thing, to sit around and do nothing all day, that's when it can swamp you.'

There was, however, one bright piece of news that cheered everybody up. With the blastings over, at least for the moment, Sara was now allowed to have a bath again.

'I can't tell you what it was like, slipping into the water,' she said. 'Absolute bliss!'

Three weeks later, Sara was admitted to hospital, and that Sunday, at church, Bill Rogers turned the thoughts, and prayers, of the whole village towards her.

'Lord, we pray that your healing love will

strengthen and sustain all those who are ill at this time. We pray for Sara Holmes, that she will be surrounded by your love.

    'Lord, in thy mercy . . .'

    'Hear our prayer.'

NINE

It was perishingly cold in the War Memorial Hall, despite the whirring of the overhead fan heaters, which over the years had become so noisy that the windows rattled, and speakers had to shout to be heard.

The Hall was built on land given by the Eggar family in memory of those who fell in the great war, and construction was supervised by Lord Baden-Powell, who for over thirty years lived at Pax Hill, a large country house lying to the west of Jenkyn Place. Baden-Powell decided that probably the person best fitted to carry out the official opening ceremony on the building's completion would be Baden-Powell, so it was the Chief Scout and hero of Mafeking himself who cut the ribbon, amidst much cheering and waving of Union Jacks, one day in 1920.

It stands right at the end of Hole Lane, beside the crossroads with the A31 and Station Road, the scene of so many of Hilda and Margaret's tea-bearing mercy dashes to injured motorists. In the mornings it is used by the mothers and toddlers of the village playgroup, during the day by the seventy-plus club, and in the evenings by the parish council, the W.I., community association and the gardening club. An experiment to create a regular social club in the bar area failed partly because so few used it, and partly because those that did drank so much that there were endless complaints of nightly drunken scenes in the car-park.

Tonight there was a meeting of the Bentley Fête and Flower Show committee, chaired by David Asher, well-known throughout the area for his talks on English nineteenth-century porcelain.

'Well, let's go on to the Donations, bearing in mind that we're looking for two to three thousand pounds to replace the marquee,' he said. This was the annual meeting to decide how to spend the proceeds of the summer fête, which this year included a spectacular three hundred and sixty pounds raised by the cowpat lottery alone; and already the committee, swathed in scarves and gloves, had agreed that the marquee which had served the village proud for nearly eighty years should within the next five years be replaced.

'We've got a request from the PCC for three hundred pounds to help repair the timbers in the church tower,' continued the chairman. 'And the Neighbourhood Watch committee have asked for twenty-five pounds towards the cost of replacing two signs in Station Road, which unfortunately have been stolen.' A few of the committee members struggled to suppress a smile. 'And there's a last-minute request, which Richard will tell us about, which involves Jim Harden, down by Bentley Green Farm, and it's a sad one.'

'You probably all know about Cherie Harden, Jim's daughter,' said Richard Leonard, the committee treasurer. 'The money is needed to help pay for flights to America, where there is the only hospital in the world where she can be treated. Tony Holmes gave me a ring about it. He said, you'll never get a letter from Jim Harden begging for money, but a contribution would be welcome.'

The sudden response of the village to their plight had astonished Jim and Cherie. The Fête and Flower Show committee was just the latest to offer help.

'The first group to approach me was the ladies' darts team, would I mind if they tried to raise a few pounds?' said Jim. 'At first I was a bit reluctant, but of course when I thought about it I gave them my blessing, and the next day they gave me a cheque for two hundred and eighty-six pounds. Then Tony and Sara Holmes offered to pay for a trip, and the girls who make the sandwiches for the village cricket team challenged the regular players to an end-of-season match, with folk sponsoring them for each run that they scored – that pulled in five hundred and fifty. Some of the farmhands at work raised a bit, so did the Rotary Club, and Tony gave permission for the local clay-pigeon shoot to use the field behind the hop-shed, and they handed over seven hundred and sixty-five pounds. Alton Lions are offering to pay for a trip, and are collecting these air-mile vouchers at garages, to try to raise enough for another.

'I'm really touched,' said Jim. 'Speechless. I don't know what to say to people. It's unbelievable.'

One of the most unexpected contributions so far had come from Bentley School, where of course Cherie had been a pupil only a few years before. The deputy head, Pat Morris, had utilized sound market principles by asking parents to sponsor their children to learn tables.

'I thought we might raise a few pounds,' said Mrs Morris. 'When we added it all up, we couldn't believe it. Five hundred and seventy pounds. Staggering.'

Cherie was managing to hold down her place on a community care training course at Alton College, although sometimes her poor speech made her difficult to understand, and her memory played tricks.

Now the College had agreed to give her time off, and Jim had booked her on to the Maryland trial.

'Absolutely fantastic,' said Cherie.

'Yes, it's good-oh,' said Jim, quietly. 'You're rarin' to go, aren't you, Cherie?'

In the front room of their cottage by the main road, Hilda and Margaret Evans were assessing the first stage of another fund-raising campaign, the crusade to rid for ever the church bell-tower of the dreaded death-watch beetle, and even they had to admit that after just a few days things were going rather well.

The target of fifty thousand pounds had at first seemed rather daunting, but already the redoubtable sisters had press-ganged a small army of helpers into service, amongst them the former postmistress, Mrs Cath Bonner, who with her husband Harvey had delivered the mail in Bentley on their bicycles for nearly twenty years, and whose son Graham had now taken over, as if by birthright.

An appeal letter had been sent to every single household in the village asking for gifts, on the grounds that even if they weren't regular churchgoers, they or their families would at some stage in their lives use the church for baptisms, weddings or funerals. There was also a massive nationwide search to track down couples who had been married at St Mary's, but who no longer lived in the area, and there was talk of a sponsored bicycle ride. Then there were the sisters' famous teas, which during the summer months were held in the churchyard for visitors to the gardens at Jenkyn Place, and which they now planned to step up dramatically to help raise funds.

'Any response yet to the parish magazine article, Hilda?' asked Margaret. They had requested people to step forward to help serve teas, or bake cakes and biscuits.

'We've had fifteen replies already, some from people who don't actually use the church, but are very keen to support us anyway.'

'How marvellous!'

'We're on the way, Margaret, we're on the way!'

Posters had also started to appear all over the village, and this morning, whilst Margaret was going up to practise the organ for a funeral, Hilda was taking an appeal poster down to the Village Stores.

She set off past the War Memorial Hall, frantically waving down the traffic that was speeding past her in the hope that some of them would slow down, and found Alan Wheatley putting up bunting in the front window of the shop.

'Morning Alan! Bung this Bell-tower Restoration Fund poster up there while you're about it, will you?'

'Morning, Miss Evans. Would you care for a glass of wine?'

Hilda looked at her watch. It was only half-past nine.

'Bit early, Alan, surely?'

'Go around the counter, Miss Evans, and you'll see.'

Around the counter stood a small group of people, obviously already quite merry as a result of a large selection of wines laid out on a table draped in starched white linen which completely blocked the aisle. Beside the bottles, there were stacks of biscuits and little heaps of cheese and pineapple. It all looked delightful.

'We're celebrating, Miss Evans! It's the shop's fiftieth anniversary!'

'Good Lord, really. Thank you so much,' said Hilda, gleefully accepting a glass. 'Cheers and good health!'

'1941, the Wheatleys came down here, Miss Evans.'

'Your grandparents?'

'That's it. Shame father couldn't see this.'

Amongst the early-morning revellers getting stuck into the wine were old Walter Sherfield, Albert Wheatley, who was Alan's uncle, Albert's sister Irene, and a handful of people from the tiny industrial estate on the other side of the main road, who usually called in early to buy sandwiches for lunchtime. Inevitably the talk was all of those early years when the Wheatley family first arrived in Bentley from their bombed-out home in the East End of London.

'It was the very first raid on London, on Saturday, 7 September 1940,' said Albert, who has a keen eye for detail coupled with an astonishing memory.

'We had a direct hit, went right down the chimney, into the cellar, blew us sky high,' said Irene, to a gripped audience. 'I was up at the church at the time, wasn't I, Albert?'

'For two days we went to various relatives in London, but they were all blown up too, so since we had friends in Bentley we came down here. On Monday, 9 September 1940.'

'We had nothing, we didn't even have a change of underwear.'

'I was actually washing in the bathroom when the air-raid siren started, on 7 September, at six o'clock. I arrived in Bentley in a vest and trousers, which I'd borrowed from some relatives.'

'It was unbelievable to wake up and listen to the birds singing, instead of the bombs raining down. A few weeks later a little lock-up hut – '

'Old First World War army hut, wasn't it? – '

'And my parents took that over, along with my sister Irene here, and that was fifty years ago this week. I think in that first week we expected to take eighty pounds; in fact we took sixty-nine pounds and five and thruppence. The rent was fourteen and six a week, and we just about made a living.'

'I remember them putting out a blackboard each morning, with carrots and potatoes and all the vegetables they'd got to sell that day,' said Walter. 'They had the old bakehouse out the back there, I remember the old steam wagon from Simmonds' in Aldershot bringing in the flour. And when the hop-pickers arrived, the bakehouse had to go flat out.'

'By the end of the first year, we'd taken over five thousand pounds, which was a lot more than anyone expected. Then in 1944 – January 1944, 31 January 1944, to be precise, exactly twenty-nine days before my twenty-first birthday, these premises became available,' said Albert. 'We grew from there. Nobody had cars then, of course, so we delivered to everybody, eleven deliveries a week, six for newspapers, three for bread deliveries, and twice a week with the mobile van. We became the first village shop in England to be converted to self-service. That was in April 1957.

Extension work started on 1 April, and was completed fifteen months later, on 23 June 1958.'

'Before the Blitz, the family had a cat-meat business,' said Alan. 'They used to go door-to-door all round the whole neighbourhood, selling cat's meat from a barrow. So who knows, without Hitler we could have been Spillers by now.'

This got a laugh from everyone, including old Mr Ratzman, who'd been a German prisoner-of-war in a camp a few miles away, and had stayed on in the village after the war.

'Congratulations, Alan, and best vishes!' said Mr Ratzman cheerily, downing his glass. 'Just keep ze prices down, vill you?'

Bentley Stores still has a big blue delivery van, driven for the last forty years by Terry Cox. His regular trips make him the darling of housebound old folk all over the outskirts of the village, and beyond. Every morning he's to be found parked on one of the myriad little country lanes which run out either side of the main road, bustling endlessly backwards and forwards to one cottage after another like some Olympic long-distance walker in training, his muscular forearms bearing countless cardboard boxes and tons of fruit and vegetables every week.

'I get their pensions, and medicines from the doctor,' says Terry. 'They're not customers, they're friends, really, aren't they? There was old Mr Masterman over at Binsted, he 'ad an 'eart-attack, so I rushed up and got the neighbour, and called the doctor. Good service, really.'

This morning, whilst the wine was flowing back in

the shop, Terry's first stop was Edy Parrot, who lived in one of Tony's cottages right beside the railway at Isington.

'Morning, Edy.'

'I've got another Royal letter this morning!' said Edy, excitedly waving a piece of paper at him. Edy's mother, eighty-eight, who started hop-picking at Glade Farm when she was four years old, was huddled by a roaring fire, and in the corner Edy's daughter was feeding a row of screaming budgerigars. A large, faded photograph of the Princess of Wales hung on the wall, prominently displayed alongside a Royal calendar several years out of date.

''Tis from 'er Majesty, this one.'

'It is?' asked Terry, with genuine interest. 'I haven't 'ad one yet!'

'I sent a card to 'er on 'er weddin' anniversary, Terry. I puts me address on the back of the envelope, as always, in case they didn't want to accept it from poor folk like us, but they did, look. "I am commanded by the Queen to write and thank you for the good wishes you sent to Her Majesty and the Duke of Edinburgh on the occasion of their Royal Ruby Wedding. Your kind message has given the Queen and His Royal Highness great pleasure." What do you think o' that, then?'

On the kitchen table Edy had laid out the four previous examples of her Royal correspondence.

'When the Duchess of York got married, I said to Mother, I've a mind to send 'er a card and 'orseshoe for 'er weddin', so I did, I gave it to the postman to take in, 'cos I couldn't get to Alton meself. Then the babies came, so that was more cards. Then there was the Queen Mum on her ninetieth.'

The Old Mill, Isington

'Very nice,' said Terry. 'Eleven pounds and a penny, love, please.'

''E does everything for us,' said Edy, as Terry strode off down the path to his van. 'Mum's pension, prescriptions, the lot. 'E likes a flutter on the 'orses, too, does Terry. When 'e goes to Goodwood, 'e puts a little bet on for us.'

Next stop was another of Tony's farm cottages, the home of old Ma Cox, Terry's aunt Daisy.

'Some of them can't get out, see, like old Daisy here,' said Terry. 'She's eighty-one, she's got a bad leg and can't walk too far.'

'Mornin' Daise, how are you?'

'Not so bad, Terry, still dragging one foot.'

'You gotta keep going, though, haven't you, Daise?'

Now Daisy has a unique claim to fame. She, along with five of her ten children, worked for Field-Marshal Lord Montgomery, partly as a housekeeper, but partly

also as a confidante and friend after the death of Monty's wife, Bettie.

Monty lived in the Old Mill at Isington, a beautiful house that was converted from two oast houses on the banks of the river, two minutes' walk from Ma Cox.

'My son Michael was Monty's chauffeur, Peter was gardener-cum-part-time chauffeur, Aileen was the housekeeper after Mrs Hunt died, along with Jean, and Pauline was the cook.

'One day Michael came and got me, and said one girl at the house refused to get up, and Monty had people coming to lunch, would I go and help? I stayed sixteen years.

'I worked there every morning, and then in the afternoon, if he was feeling lonely, he used to say to Michael, go up and get your mother, I want to have a talk. He was a very lonely man, after his wife died. He talked about his war experiences. He said to me one day, do people like me? I said, well, I expect a lot of people do. He said, people say that I killed people. I said, well, you did, didn't you, in that one battle, a lot of people died. Yes, he said, but I had to lose a hundred to save a thousand. I don't think that was wrong, do you?'

Monty gave Ma Cox a photograph, of a visit he made late in life to one of the wartime cemeteries in Sicily.

'Did I kill all those people? he asked me when he gave it to me. I said, well I don't know, really. He was never well again, not after that visit.

'We were friends, he was a good friend. I'd lost my husband, and I was lonely, too. Both the same kind of people, you see. If he said he wanted something done, he wanted it done, and I'm the same. We used to talk about the Government a lot, and even though he was great friends with Mr Churchill, we agreed on that, too. Vote Labour, he said, and so did I.

'One birthday he gave me ten pounds. I said I'm going to save that, for my fur coat. He said, haven't you got a fur coat? Every lady should have a fur coat. I said no, so he gave me the money to go and buy one. He gave me a box of French soap too – still got it upstairs – a silk headscarf, and then there's the Toby Jug.'

The huge Toby Jug takes pride of place on Ma Cox's sideboard. It's of Monty's head and shoulders, clad in his army greatcoat, the Sword of State by his side, and his great beret forming the jug's lip. Only two were made by Royal Doulton, and both were given to the Field-Marshal in his honour. One was smashed, and Monty gave the other to Ma Cox.

'It'll be safe with you,' he had said.

Back at the shop, over yet another glass of wine, they'd been sharing memories of Monty, too. From behind the counter, Alan Wheatley used to see him regularly, once a week.

'The Field-Marshal used to be driven up here in his Daimler – it was a Daimler, wasn't it, Walter?'

'Daimler or a Rolls – '

'A big flag on the front, of course, and he used to pull up outside the shop, dead on nine o'clock on a Thursday morning, to draw his pension. Always first in the queue.'

'I remember him coming up the church,' said Walter. 'One Sunday he came along, and asked the rector if he could have his own special seat on one of the front pews, and the rector said, we don't have any special seats at Bentley Church, so he never came again. He liked his own way, Monty did.'

TEN

It was turning out to be something of a celebration for Denise and Kevin. Denise's parents were there, and so was her sister Julie, and everyone ended up laughing a good deal, drinking their health, and wishing them a long and happy life in Bentley. It was like being married all over again.

They were at the Jolly Farmer, down the road at Blacknest, for the annual skittles tournament between the parents and staff of the village school. The teachers, under the formidable leadership of Pat Morris, the deputy head, were in buoyant mood.

'I got six down out of nine, which isn't bad, but I come from a cricketing family and they'd be very ashamed of me. Come on, we'll do better, Phil, grab the ball!' said Mrs Morris, beaming. She's a dynamic lady, much prone to beaming, her ruddy face topped by a fine crop of grey hair, and she had been in love with teaching for years.

'Some parent just said to me, can I call you Pat, since this is a social occasion, and I said, look, you call

me Pat anytime, for God's sake. I taught young Denise
here. And Julie. And Angela. And Tracy.'

'And Karen,' said Mrs Thompson, Denise's
mother.

'And Karen, because Mrs Thompson only pro-
duces daughters, but her daughters have now produced
sons as well, so now I'm teaching them too!'

'I think it's very nice Mrs Morris still speaks to us,'
said Julie.

'Pat!' said Mrs Morris.

'You frightened the life out of us, you know, at
school!'

'My Karen, who's now in Australia, she used to
come home and say, oh Mrs Morris, she did shout
today!' said Mrs Thompson, screaming with laughter,
and a small group of interested parents gathered
around them. This was the kind of exchange that rarely
happened within the school walls.

'I don't think that fear does any harm at all,' said
Mrs Morris, defiantly. 'Are you proud of your children,
Mrs Thompson?'

'Oh yes. They're all right. You did a good job on
them.'

'Thank you very much!'

The evening at the Jolly Farmer was also something of a landmark for the locals. It was almost exactly
a year since most of the main part of the pub had been
destroyed after a massive explosion and fire, followed
by one of the biggest police investigations the county
has ever seen.

Of course, it had caused a sensation, and to this
day no-one can be sure of exactly what happened. They
thought at first it was a gas explosion, caused by a
build-up of calor gas just outside the kitchen. Later,

when police forensic experts arrived, they discovered that the fire had been started deliberately. There was evidence of quantities of petrol having been poured around the building, although no clues as to how it was set alight.

Twelve hours after the explosion, they found the body of one of the pub's chefs in the rubble. Despite a major investigation, involving thousands of house-to-house enquiries throughout that part of North Hampshire, the circumstances surrounding the death remain an unsolved mystery.

Only the skittle-alley remained unscathed by the blast, and the school had been keen to book it for tonight's match as a gesture of support for the re-opening of the Jolly Farmer, even though there were fears amongst the pub's neighbours that whoever had carried out the first attack might now return for a second attempt.

Tonight, though, the parents were smiling – they had thrashed the teachers and prised the trophy from their reluctant fingers, much to Mrs Morris' chagrin. They had raised some money for the school too, which with the introduction of the National Curriculum was needed more than ever.

Rather like Mrs Morris, and perhaps because of her, the village school was fizzing with activity, with a renewed sense of purpose. It had first opened its doors to the village children in 1842, and now Mrs Morris and the newly-installed head, Phil Callaway, were hoping to track down the school's oldest living pupil to open a Grand Victorian Fête to celebrate the school's 150th anniversary. With two big new housing estates in the village and the closing of the village school nearby at Froyle, Bentley School had recently been completely renovated, and was enjoying a new lease of life. Nearly everyone, rich and poor, sent their children to Bentley School.

'What do you think about writing to Roger Royle, to see if he'll come and help judge the Reading Competition?' Mrs Morris suggested, in a flash of inspiration.

'Roger Royle? The TV vicar?'

'He's just been appointed as chaplain to the Lord Mayor Treloar College, up at Froyle.'

'Let's give him a go,' said Mr Callaway. 'Why not?'

The night, though, really went to Kevin and Denise, who hadn't stopped grinning all evening.

'I never really had the confidence in myself, to think that I was any good,' said Kevin. 'It's quite a good feeling.'

'I really think, deep down, neither of us could have faced moving,' said Denise. 'It's smashing, the end of one chapter and the beginning of another.'

So Kevin would be here next year to light the school bonfire, after all.

In a small, well-equipped office just behind the village stores, the Bentley and Froyle Oil Company was having another frantic day, buying and selling crude oil on the international markets for shipment all over the world.

The Bentley and Froyle Oil Company consists of a teletext screen, a telex, a fax, a telephone, a desk, and one man, John Dobson, formerly of the mighty Shell Oil Company. In the mornings, in term-time at least, he can rely on Clare Asher, wife of the Fête and Flower

Show committee chairman, to come in and help with the paperwork. Apart from that, he works alone.

John considers the decision to launch his own company and base it in the wilds of North Hampshire, to have been an inspiration, although at the time many of his former colleagues in the business sincerely believed he had completely lost his marbles.

'A lot of people moved out of New York into Houston, which through the boom was expensive, although Houston is now quite cheap. Today the oil business really hinges on London, Houston and Singapore, so I plumped for Bentley, which is cheaper than all three.

'At first I worried it may have been a disadvantage to be working out here in the country, but in fact most people envy me, because they'd all much rather work two miles away from home, and have the freedom to come to the office in jeans and sneakers.'

In front of his desk, John has a screen which keeps him up to date on the movements of all world commodity prices, and allows him to monitor the prices of crude oil and oil products in the futures markets. Besides that there's a television, which he uses partly to keep an eye on exchange rates and non-instantaneous changes in world oil prices, but which mainly in summer keeps him up to date on ball-by-ball television coverage of the Test Matches. Beside that is a huge, gurgling aquarium full of tropical fish, which keeps him amused when the markets are quiet, or when rain stops play.

John Dobson, in his forties and with just that hint of an expanding waistline that were he in a grey suit would immediately tell you he was a successful businessman, had his feet up on the desk, and was still on the telephone, as he had been most of the afternoon.

There were rumours of changes on the North Sea Eko-fisk platform which could dramatically affect his current deal, but his cool and calculated analysis of the situation gave not the smallest suggestion of panic, or even of mild concern.

'I'm managing a cargo of crude for one of my clients which is loading in Nigeria at the end of next week: 920,000 barrels, the biggest size that comes out of Nigeria.

'It looks as though there's a gross profit on offer of 180,000–200,000 dollars, although sometimes these cargoes can lose a million dollars, or, as during the Gulf War, more than two million.

'I think – only think, mind you – that an announcement is due this afternoon, or Monday morning, which could affect the immediate future production of the Ekofisk field, and therefore world prices. Our documentation for the Nigeria shipment, and our letter of credit, has to be ready by Monday at the latest, so we have to make a decision about altering the price of our cargo before then.

'If we guess the Ekofisk announcement the wrong way, we could be losing our profit completely, instead of maybe doubling it. Even a change of ten cents per barrel could alter the profit by 90–100,000 dollars.'

He picked up his remote control unit, and zapped off all the screens, one by one, like a sharpshooter picking off tin cans on top of a wall.

'Blow it,' he said, or words to that effect. 'Time for a little refreshment with George.'

He drove in his BMW out onto the main road, up past the War Memorial Hall, past the long, winding driveway which leads to Baden-Powell's beloved Pax Hill, now a nursing home, and took the next right, to the Prince of Wales at Froyle, close by his home.

As well as being chairman of the Bentley village cricket club, John is a fanatical member of the Prince of Wales Golfing Society, founded by the genial Scots landlord of the pub, George Farquharson, who's famous throughout the area for producing a high-octane Rum Toft for his annual Burns Night celebration.

This evening there was a great air of festivity in the bar which, even at this early hour, was already full of golfers, toasting a remarkable feat by their treasurer, Hector. He'd won the eternal admiration of everyone in the pub by scoring two holes-in-one in successive games, and was now in the corner of the bar downing pints and being interviewed by Annette Booth, the village correspondent of the *Farnham Herald*.

'I was playing with the boys at one of our monthly games down in Winchester,' said Hector Gilchrist, another Scotsman. 'We were at the third hole, one hundred and eighty-eight yards, so I took a five iron. The guy we were with said, all you have to do is just hit the ball up, fade it up and over the hill which obscured the pin, and it'll go down the hole, so that's exactly what I did. It was easy.

'The trouble was that none of us knew it had gone down, so we all spent some time looking for the ball before we found it. Back at the clubhouse, of course, I was expected to buy a round, which was a bit of a drawback.'

'We all noticed you spent rather a long time in the shower,' said John.

'What was the second occasion?' asked Annette, scribbling furiously.

'The second time was the very next time I played, on the back nine at Hindhead. It was the short fifteenth, so this time I could see it.'

'It must be pleasant, actually to see it go in the hole.'

'Yes, and I'd been playing so badly I knew I'd be embarrassed to put my card in, so it was a nice feeling. I put it down to years of drinking good quality malt Scotch.'

John Dobson was wide-eyed with envy.

'It's totally unbelievable. I was behind him when he did the second one, and when I heard them all say, it's another hole-in-one, we all said rubbish, that's not possible. Somebody said the chance of you getting a hole-in-one once during a lifetime is about thirty thousand-to-one, and thirty-thousand times thirty-thousand is a lot of millions-to-one chance that you'd do it twice,' said John, who was used to dealing in large figures. 'To do it twice in two rounds is simply out-rageous. One of life's unexpected moments of pure joy. And very expensive.'

Then, after a photograph for the local paper, Hec-tor stood and cleared his throat, and it became immediately apparent to all why George had already cannily booked him to perform at the forthcoming Burns Night Supper.

> Oh, that little white pill,
> Went a-rollin' down the hill,
> And rolled right into the bunker . . .

sang Hector, in a magnificent tenor voice, his forefinger stuck firmly into his right ear.

> From there to the green,
> I took sixteen,
> And then, by Gosh! I sunk her!

After the applause had died down, George took John out to the back of the bar, and into the cellar.

'Here, John, you're an oilman, stick your finger in that, and see what ye make of it!'

This was George's Rum Toft, a concoction he meticulously brews every year. The whole process starts in July, when he lays down the strawberries, mixed with sugar and rum, in a large earthenware jar. He then waits for the next picking, the raspberries, and with those creates the next layer, followed by pea-ches, nectarines, apricots, and finally plums, all hand picked and personally selected by George himself from the organic farm run by Geoff Groves and his wife, down in the village. Once it's full the lid is sealed and the toft is stored at a constant, cool temperature in George's cellar, until it's required at the end of January.

It was the rum itself, though, which had made George's explosive creation something of a local legend. He had managed to secure some of the old Navy rum, 151° proof, which officially should have been disposed of when the Royal Navy abolished the daily tot twenty years ago, but which was miraculously still in circulation, despite never having been subject to Customs duty. George was always a little vague on his sources of supply.

A look of sheer ecstasy passed across John's face.

'God, that's good,' he sighed.

'You'll be a-comin' to Burns Night again yourself, John?'

'You try and keep me away, George.'

'Let's hope we're not raided by the Customs men. There might just be a knock at the door, just as we're getting stuck in!'

Poor Jim Harden was looking like the victim of some revolting medieval plague. His face and hands were covered in huge black scabs, prompting a maddening internal battle over the urge to scratch. He hadn't been to work at Glade Farm for over a week.

He had caught chickenpox, which was raging through the school. Cherie had never had the disease, so reluctantly he had packed her off at high speed to her mother's home near Camberley. This was a pity, because it was the eve of Cherie's eighteenth birthday, and the following day she was off to America.

The treatment was to take three days, but Cherie would be out in Maryland for a full week, staying at a purpose-built accommodation unit by the hospital called the Children's Inn, where Cherie's mother could stay, too. The proposal was to administer a slightly different drug regime to each candidate on the trial, and then by a series of liver biopsies over several months, monitor the cholesterol levels, and by comparison, the most effective drug regime would eventually emerge. This could then become the standard treatment for the disease.

It was a long, arduous programme with no guarantee of success, but now at least it looked as though Cherie could afford to see it through. Money was still coming in; only last week he had received the proceeds of a plant sale at Jenkyn Place, and one of the villagers had given Jim two complimentary tickets he had been offered by an airline.

'You got my card? There are three or four others here,' he said to Cherie, over the telephone. 'I won't be there to see you off, because of the chickenpox, so have a good trip. All the best then, babe, see you when you come back. 'Bye.'

ELEVEN

The panel of judges, sitting alone now in the school hall, were facing a difficult decision.

In the centre of the table was the towering figure of the Revd Roger Royle. Beside him was Anne Joy, the chairman of the school Governors, who lived in the lovely Tudor house at Marelands opposite the school, where Gilbert White had been a frequent visitor. On the other side of Mr Royle sat the small, dapper, moustached face of Lieutenant-General Sir William Pike, late of the Royal Artillery, well-known local benefactor, for many years chairman of the Fête and Flower Show committee, and Mrs Joy's predecessor as chairman of the Governors.

'Stephanie made very good use of the word "wobble" – actually they were all good on "wobble",' said Mr Royle. 'Sir William, what about Sarah Bennington, the last girl?'

Throughout the morning they had listened to dozens of children recite a story about Jumbo Brown and his friends Duck, Rabbit, and Little Bear, in the annual reading competition, the brainchild of Sir William.

'I've been a school governor for over twenty-five years, ever since I retired from the Army. I come in one day a week, to hear the two top forms read, and then I have a short chat to them, because in many ways breaking the ice with adults is as important as reading. A few years ago, I thought, why shouldn't I give a prize to the children who read the best?'

Now the children were waiting in their classrooms for the announcement of the winner.

'Sarah's a very sweet little girl, and I think she was very accurate.'

'I think she's also had deportment classes,' said Roger Royle. 'I mean, did you see the way she walked in? And none of them had shaky hands, did they?'

'Yes, they were all supremely confident. Not easy, is it?'

After a time, coffee was brought in.

'I hear you used to listen to pupils reading at Treloar's, Sir William. I look at your College portrait frequently.'

'Very kind of you. I had to stop eventually, due to age. Of course, I see you mostly on the television.'

'Not any more. Only radio now, which is much more respectable. You get nicer people on radio.'

'Also you can hear what they're saying so much better on radio. Why is that?'

The debate over the reading resumed, and it soon emerged that the majority of the judges favoured Millie Hume, the daughter of Stuart Hume, who had replaced old Walter Sherfield as head gardener of Jenkyn Place.

'I thought Millie stood well, and had a very intelligent delivery,' said Mr Royle.

The Village School

'I would be happy with Millie,' added Sir William.

'Do we all go for Millie then?'

'Millie and Sarah Bennington are what I call clinical readers,' said Mrs Joy.

'I disagree with you on the "clinical", I really felt there was more to it.'

At last the children were called back into the school hall. Roger Royle launched into a summing-up speech.

'Eugene, I thought you read the piece about the jumble sale very well; you obviously have a close affiliation with jumble sales! Stephanie and Nina and Sarah and Millie, you all obviously loved the piece you were reading, and wanted us to love it as well. But the winner is Millie Hume.'

As the applause died down, Mr Royle continued.

'Reading will sustain you in life. The television won't, the video will go dead on you, the machines will break up. Reading will be the thing you'll get so much

from, it will add to your imagination, and it'll take you out into a wider world. It'll help you cope with loneliness, because when you're on your own, as you will be at some time or other, if you can pick up a book, you'll enter a different world.'

In the end, they all thought Roger Royle had done rather well, and Mrs Morris was congratulated for coming up with such a fine idea.

The initial response to the Bell-tower Restoration Fund was overwhelming. Within the first few months, nearly thirty thousand pounds had come in, mainly through gifts and convenants, much more than even the most optimistic estimates from such a God-fearing community. It even looked as if there might be enough funds to give the magnificent old organ its rather overdue twenty-year clean-up, and now the search was on for suitable builders to place the main contract with.

More exciting news had come from Winchester. Bishop Colin, who had so far never visited the parish, had accepted an invitation to preach at the big Flower Festival which the Parochial Church Council had planned for twelve months hence, to celebrate the successful completion of the building works. With the Bishop booked, other participants would be easier to secure. The Guildford Cathedral Choir had been asked to appear, and every single organisation in the village, from the Scouts and Guides and Women's Institute to the county police and even the doctor's surgery opposite Babs Field, was to be asked to contribute to the floral displays.

It was going to be a great occasion.

Two weeks into the New Year came the news from Glade Farm that everyone had been silently expecting and dreading.

Sara Carlton Holmes, who had won the respect and admiration of the whole village as she fought against her illness, died at home, after being brought back from hospital for Christmas. She was forty-eight years old.

All the family were there, of course, Chris, Sally, Pom and Fogs, and when Maureen and Eileen arrived for work in the morning, Tony told them that Sara had finally passed away in the early hours of the morning. He said they could go home, but they chose to stay.

Even though all of them, including Sara, had known she was dying, the news was still difficult to accept.

'She was such a tremendous personality,' said her old friend Mrs Coke, down in Jenkyn Place. 'You felt this warmth when she was around, the fun, she enjoyed life. She and Tony were such a wonderful couple. It must have made such tremendous happiness for him, after losing his first wife. They were married sixteen or seventeen years.

'One realised the illness was very serious, but she was young and full of life, and one simply couldn't believe it was true. Even when she died, I didn't really realise how ill she was. She had tremendous courage, right to the end, and carried on farming and looking after her cows. It was wonderful. One regrets not having done more to help, not having seen her more. It's always too late, which is so sad.'

Sara's funeral took place in the churchyard of St Mary's, and the following day there was a memorial service. Nobody could remember the Church more full; there was standing room only.

The family spent a good deal of time choosing the prayers and hymns they felt Sara would have wanted, and because of that the service became more of a rousing celebration than an occasion to mourn. There was '*Jerusalem*' and '*We Plough The Fields And Scatter*'; and Sara's favourite hymn, '*Glory, Glory, Alleluia!* which is not what the villagers usually expected to sing at a funeral.

Mine eyes have seen the glory of the coming of the Lord;
He is trampling out the vintage where the grapes of wrath are stored,
He hath loosed the fateful lightning of his terrible swift sword,
His truth is marching on!

Glory, glory, alleluia!
Glory, glory, alleluia!
His truth is marching on.

The old timbers rattled in the bell-tower as the rousing chorus rang out.

The address was given by another old friend, and a fellow breeder of Sara's beloved Dexter cattle, the Revd John Shorrock, who knew Tony and Sara from the cattle show circuit.

'As I walked into this crowded church to take my part in the service I seemed to hear Sara's voice,' the Revd Shorrock told the congregation. "That's how to do it, John! You spend your life trying to get 'em into church and I've got them here, no effort!"

'Sara celebrated life every moment she had of it. She praised the King of Heaven, her creator, in the way she lived life, and passed that on to the rest of us. Brimming over with an energy only a few seem to possess, she was full of Spirit – Holy Spirit, because the energy she had can only come from Him, the Creator and Sustainer of our being.

'At the shows last summer, Sara bounded about, looking great and enjoying every minute she could, instead of giving into the illness which was sapping her energy and making its terrible demands on her brave spirit.

'This service will help you and me to celebrate life as Sara did. Try to keep up with her – she set us all a splendid pace.'

In the beauty of the lilies Christ was born across the sea,

With a glory in his bosom that transfigures you
  and me:
As he died to make men holy, let us live to make
  men free,
While God is marching on.
Glory, glory, alleluia!

TWELVE

At the end of February, Brian and Henry could be seen out again at first light in the hop-gardens, moving slowly against the wintry skyline from one plant to another, each bearing fifteen-foot poles for stringing up, and sometimes wearing dark glasses to shield their eyes from the blinding low-angle sun.

The plants are still dormant, the withered brown shoots a mere remnant of last year's crop, but beneath the frosty earth their roots are preparing to explode into life. Beside each one, there's a metal ring corkscrewed into the ground where one end of the string is secured; then, using the pole like a giant needle, the string is threaded through a second ring attached to the wirework high above, and back down to the next plant. It is a laborious process which can be completed at high speed only with great skill, and when there is virtually no wind.

Later, round about Easter, when the new fragile green shoots have appeared, the men will be back, sometimes with casual labour, this time to train each plant around its string, to help it reach upwards, following the sun. A watchful eye is kept on those who haven't done the job before; the shoot must be trained clockwise, not as your instinct would tell you, like a runner-bean, anti-clockwise, or it'll die. According to custom, the plants should have reached the top of the wirework by 21 June, Midsummer's Day.

This is the time, too, to keep a vigilant eye for first signs of the red spider mite. Because they're too small to see, the trick is to sprinkle a little fine soil on the underside of a leaf. Any particles that remain after shaking the soil off will reveal the existence of the spider's tiny web. It could be another difficult season ahead; once again, there had been no substantial snowfall over the winter months.

Elsewhere, the corn had been given its top-dressing of fertiliser, the hedges had been cut, as always, before the birds had a chance to select a nesting spot, and, much to the delight of old Walter in particular, the evenings were starting to draw out. Walter had been walking over his vegetable patch every day for the last few weeks and today, for the first time, the mud hadn't stuck to the bottom of his boots – the sign he'd been looking for that the soil was now dry enough after the ravages of the winter to start preparing his seed beds. 'Sow early peas and broad beans into boxes now for transplanting in March if ground conditions are suitable,' Walter had said in his Gardening Hints column in the parish magazine, and it was looking as though his advice this year would be about right. 'Prune newly planted blackcurrant bushes, and gooseberry and redcurrant bushes. Cut back all shoots to about four or five buds. Plant new rose bushes.'

This evening, though, he'd put the fork away early, and set about smartening himself up to go out. Walter always wore a shirt and tie, even in the garden, but now he'd dusted down his suit and put on his trilby, and Jessie was wearing her prettiest dress.

They locked up the cottage and set off at a leisurely pace down Toad Hole Lane, towards the War Memorial Hall where the coach would be waiting to take them to Alton. Jessie was pleased that Walter had even considered walking; he had had heart trouble recently and found walking a struggle, which is why she had booked a week in Worthing for their summer holiday. Worthing, she'd been told, was very flat.

This was a Bentley Gardening club outing, and as its president, old Walter was its senior member. He had been looking forward to it for months, partly because he and Jess rarely got out much these days, and partly because they were to be the guests of Alton Horticultural Society, whose own president was none other than the gardening expert, Alan Titchmarsh, tonight's speaker.

'I've never met the man, but I read his gardening column in the paper, so I'd be keen to meet him,' said Walter.

'He's on the television, too, isn't he Walt?'

'Yes, and there are some things I don't always agree with, same as when Percy Thrower was top man,' said the man who'd managed Jenkyn Place's famous gardens for forty years. 'He used to say, I'm putting in these cuttings this week, I'll show you how to put 'em in. Next week's programme, he says, here's those cuttings I put in last week, I'm ready now to pot 'em up. When you've only got a cold greenhouse you just can't get cuttings on in a week. Three or four weeks, maybe.'

'How are you, Walter?' asked Alan Sorsby, the chairman, who lives in John O'Pease Cottage, between Jenkyn Place and the Church. They were all in the coach, speeding down towards Alton.

'Oh, not so's you'd grumble,' said Walter.

'What's all this about ghosthunters at Jenkyn Place?'

'I don't know anything about that, Alan. I never saw anything, not in all the years I worked there, that's for sure. I tell you what, though. In the Lawsons' time, I used to go down and milk the cows of an evening, and I had a big bucket to put the milk in, and a big cloth around the bucket, and a white coat on. I used to go up through the steps there, across the little bridge at Jenkyn Place and over the road. I'd just got on the bridge one night – it was a bright, moonlit night – carrying this bucket, with the white overall on, and all the Lilliwhites' hop-pickers was a-comin down to the village. I heard 'em say, oh my God, there's the ghost, there's the White Lady, and they scooted back up the hill, and round by the church, and they never come that way again. It was me they'd seen, see!'

The Community Centre at Alton was packed, and Walter and Jessie just managed to squeeze in at the back, which was a pity because Walter had hoped he might meet Alan Titchmarsh after the talk. Back here he'd no doubt be lost amongst all those hoping to snatch a word about their own gardening problems with the speaker before he left.

'Any people here who were interested in gardening when they were children? If so, you're very odd,' said Alan Titchmarsh, who was launching into his talk armed with a battery of colourful slides and an apparently inexhaustible supply of gardening anecdotes.

'I was told I was odd, because I started very, very tiny, and I've got a picture of myself standing in my grandfather's allotment, aged about two and a half. Football didn't hold much attraction for me.'

The builders had started to move into the church, erecting a little mobile office in the car-park, and swathing the bell-tower in scaffolding. The Revd Rogers had written out for them a week-by-week timetable of church activities, in the optimistic hope that they might be able to time their tea-breaks so that services could continue undisturbed by hammering and drilling.

It was now apparent that the original estimate of £50,000 for the work might not be sufficient, so the indefatigable Hilda Evans was rallying the troops for another money-spinning wheeze – a sponsored bicycle-ride.

This involved volunteers collecting money for cycling around as many churches as possible in the deanery of Alton between ten in the morning and six in the evening. This was quite a challenge since the deanery consists of more than its fair share of hills and dales, and boasts no less than thirty-three churches, many of them, out in the country areas, rarely used, and very isolated. Some older people, unable to face pedalling on bikes, were going to earn a few pounds by walking around some of the churches, and some even intended to do the circuit on horseback. Half the money would go to the Historic Churches Trust, half to the bell-tower fund.

Sally, behind the Post Office counter in the Village Stores, had agreed to hand out sponsorship forms to customers, but was stoutly resisting considerable pressure from Hilda to participate.

'I've got to work that day, Miss Evans.'

'I know you cycle, because I saw you cycling on Sunday morning!'

'It's only got three gears, Miss Evans.'

'My bike's only got three gears, that's more than enough!'

'Difficult to change the rota for that day, Miss Evans.'

Hilda left a pile of sponsorship forms on the counter, and on her way out bumped into Cath Bonner, who with her husband, Harvey, had a big advantage over other riders because for over twenty years they had been spending all day cycling around the village delivering the mail.

'We reckon we've cycled the equivalent of three times around the world,' Cath would say. 'For twenty years, apart from holidays, we only ever had six days off work between the two of us. He'd do eleven miles every day, and I'd do seven. That's a lot of miles.' When the Bonners had eventually retired, the Stores organised a fund to give them a farewell gift, and within a few weeks £1400 had been raised.

At seventy-two Hilda was no mean rider herself. Last year on the ride, she got round twenty-one churches in over forty-four miles, and this year she planned to do better.

'Planned your route yet, Cath?'

'Graham, my son, he says he's coming with us this year, and he says we're going round the lot!'

'Good heavens!'

'I'm starting at Bentley, then on to Binsted, Kingsley, Worldham, Oakhanger, and then Selborne, East Tistead, and so on, back to Bentley.'

'Well I plan to take the train down to Alton and

work backwards, although I'm cutting out Lasham and Fordham, because for each one you have to climb up a hill for about half an hour, and that's just a waste of energy,' said Hilda, who'd spent some time working on her plan. 'Also, it'll seem like going home all the way!'

U p at Glade Farm, it was impossible not to notice that the house, so used to echoing to the sound of heated discussion over the latest cattle-showing rules or ear-tagging techniques, amidst frequent, raucous laughter, now lay strangely silent.

Tony had been amazed to receive more than 600 letters following Sara's death, many from people he could scarcely remember, some from people he'd never heard of. He needed a change, but he couldn't face Cornwall and the holiday cottage where he and Sara had shared so many happy times.

Now he made an impulsive decision. There was time enough ahead of them to re-assess their future, and discuss how best to manage the farm. In the meantime, he decided to take the girls to Paris for a long weekend, leaving Chris to look after things at home.

'They deserve a break,' he said. 'And as for me – well, I shall probably go to the Folies Bergère, eat too much and drink too much. Why not? You can't take it with you when you go.'

═══ **THIRTEEN** ═══

'How very, very nice to meet you,' said Alan Titchmarsh, shaking Walter firmly by the hand. Walter was glowing with delight. 'So you were one of the gardeners at Jenkyn Place! Coo!'

'Thirty-seven years. I retired in 1978 at the age of seventy.'

'And you were the head gardener? It's got an amazing reputation, that place, hasn't it?' Alan was clearly impressed.

'I started in 1931. There were four of us then.'

'Do you remember what you were paid?'

'Twenty-nine and thruppence a week. Nine pence insurance. Thirty bob a week.'

'I didn't get much more than that when I was in Yorkshire. I got three pounds five and thruppence.'

'We had people called McConnell there then. We had these herbaceous borders – you seen those?'

'Yes!'

'I made those, in September 1931, and we'd got a bit of a dry summer. Old Mrs McConnell said to the then head gardener, ask the men to come back after tea and water the borders. We said, yes, we'd do it for a shilling an hour, which wasn't much overtime, then. Oh, she said, I couldn't think of that, she said!'

'Did they get watered?'

'Had to do it the next day! She wouldn't pay out! Then I remember old Tom Neal, and his onions, getting ready for the village show. Tom was showing well, and so was his neighbour, old Jimmy Munday. Tom Neal had four good onions, and he wanted two more. So he got up early Saturday morning, up Mr Eggar's garden, and was just pulling up a pair o' good 'uns when who should appear, but R.B. Eggar himself. You stealing my onions, Neal? says he. Well, sir, I'm just making up my six for the Show, he said.

'Later on, Mr Eggar, who was president of the show, had to give out the prizes. He was announcing the class for the best six onions, and read out old Tom Neal's name. Bit embarrassing, really, but not a word was said.'

'Do you garden in your spare time, now you're retired?' asked Alan quickly, as Walter took a deep breath and looked set to launch into yet another anecdote.

'I do me own garden – and I'm eighty-three next Sunday!'

'There's hope for me yet then, Walter,' said Alan Titchmarsh.

Walter would be dining out on that, for some time to come.

Margaret Evans stood by the door of the church, looking rather like a race official with her pen and clipboard poised at the ready. She'd hidden the thermos flask just behind one of the pews, and on the table, beside the piles of unsold parish magazines, was a large jug of lemonade.

'Good luck, dear!' she said to Cath Bonner, who was setting off at high speed beneath the arms of the great yew, down the cobbled pathway through the churchyard.

'I'll see you later!'

'Don't do too many, we can't afford all that sponsorship money!'

Margaret would be on station all day, signing off the cyclists as they arrived, one by one, after sweating up Hole Lane and past Jenkyn Place. There'd be other Margarets at most of the other thirty-two churches dotted all over the Deanery; at the more isolated churches the pen and clipboard, and jug of pop, would be left unattended, and here the signatures of the cyclists themselves would be the only safeguard against fraud.

The cyclists all seemed to be doing the round by different routes, which meant that they'd be passing each other in opposite directions, making it marginally more interesting than all going in one great convoy. Margaret had already waved off one of the churchwardens, the choirmaster Patrick Hodson, and now here was Giles Harrap, the son of Colonel Harrap from Marsh House, St Mary's other churchwarden. Giles is a barrister and famous for his manic commentaries for the donkey derby and bale-throwing competitions at the fête. This morning he'd arrived with his brother John and nephew Richard, all knobbly-kneed, plastered with reflective safety flashes, and keen as mustard.

'After Oakhanger, Selborne and Newton Valence,

we hope to meet up with Mummy and Gilbert with the lunch,' said Giles. 'Toodle-oo!'

'You must be John?' asked Margaret.

'Yes, I came down from London this morning, by car, to be with Giles and Richard, as this is such fun! Bye-eee!'

Twenty miles away, a slightly red-faced Hilda had now reached East Tistead, having knocked off the seven churches in the Alton area where she had arrived by train, with her bicycle in the guard's van. She paused for a moment and took a swig of pop from the bottle in her knapsack. It was quite warm and breezy, and the going was easier than she'd anticipated, thanks in part to Harvey Bonner's thorough overhaul of her old bicycle.

There were already seventeen signatures on the list at the church, including another Evans she didn't know, and after a short pause in the gloom to catch her breath, Hilda was off again in the sunshine, a lonely figure puffing slowly through the picturesque rolling landscape between East Tistead and Farringdon, heading out past the watercress meadows to hamlets that felt as isolated as any she'd ever visited.

The Chequers is thought to be the oldest pub in Hampshire to hold a recorded liquor licence. Close to the Pilgrims' Way, and a few yards from an ancient well, there's been a hostelry of some sort on the site for centuries, although the present building dates back to 1572, when the regulars at the bar would no doubt mull over the latest Elizabethan gossip.

The Chequers was always a favourite with the hop-pickers, and in old Mr Bundy's day the place was never closed, the windows being the main method of entry and exit when the police were about and he was obliged to lock the door. Then a Frenchman took over, and in the process of renovation discovered that the old barrels of sherry which had stood unopened and gently sweating for so long behind the bar had formed stalactites of solid alcohol through the floorboards, and into the roof of the cellar below.

With the newcomer came a dashing French menu; the old yard at the front was furnished with rough-hewn oak benches, and a vine was established to form a shady roof; and suddenly the pub became fashionable. In the summer sunshine, with Shetland ponies grazing behind, the smell of garlic from the kitchens and bunches of red grapes above, you could for all the world be in Provence. There had only ever been one bar – none of this quaint English custom of dividing the drinkers into 'lounge' and 'public' – but now more than ever the Chequers became a place where retired admirals and QCs could be found chatting with dustmen, or aircrew from the helicopter base at Odiham, and even businessmen from London appeared occasionally at lunch, seeking a breath of country air and a discreet corner to share a few stolen hours with their secretaries.

These days the Chequers, back in the very English hands of Chris Phillips and his young manager Hugh, who between opening hours manages Bentley's Venture Scouts, has become the haunt of many of the village's tending-towards-the-upwardly-mobile young set. At lunch the average age is still sixty, but in the evenings it's scarcely over twenty, all ages drawn by a selection of food not typical of quiet Hampshire pubs. The bar menu includes scrambled eggs with smoked salmon and fresh daily seafood from Billingsgate; the

The Chequers

restaurant menu, created by a wild Australian gourmet called Francis who can't resist anything new, is a cross-section of English, French, Thai and Cajun food, most of it laced with a few drops from the six cases of cooking wine produced from the vine, religiously trod at the end of every season by the unclad feet of the landlord and his young manager.

Today Chris Holmes had dragged his father Tony out for a pint although, as is the way in these things, it was Tony who was expected to buy the round of drinks.

Tony was quietly relieved to get out of the house. Maureen was there every morning, leaving at noon after putting a spud in the oven for his lunch, but Fogs was back at boarding school, Sally and Pom had returned to their lives in London, and Glade House seemed bigger and emptier than ever. At least Pom

managed to get home for most weekends: part of her business studies course at Oxford Polytechnic was to spend a year working unpaid for the United Nations Association in London and Tony was always delighted to see her; she looked, and spoke, so like Sara, and reminded him so much of her.

'Evening Mr Holmes. Bit wet, isn't it?' said Hugh.

'We need it,' said Tony. 'Anyway, if it's wet outside, get wet inside, I say. Ideal place to be on a day like this. Glasses with handles, please. I hate straight glasses, I positively loathe them! Why is that?'

'You think you get better value for money from a jug, because its heavier.'

'What do I owe you?'

'To you, Mr Holmes, five pounds.'

'Five pounds! Beer can't be that expensive, can it?

It's only water, hops and barley!'

Suddenly, these looked like being hard times for Glade Farm. After years of prosperity, when farming a large acreage coupled with low interest rates meant endless smiles from the bank manager and easy access to bank loans, the climate had chilled. Tony's father and grandfather would never have believed it possible, but the truth was that British farmers were producing too much food; an irony not lost on Chris, who sat, fuming with frustration, watching news bulletins bursting with pictures of huge bread queues, and sometimes riots, amongst the hungry millions only a few hundred miles away in Eastern Europe.

Worse still, Sara's death at so young an age had produced very high death duties, which the family were totally unprepared for, and could not meet so long as things stayed just as they'd always been.

With Tony still emotionally reeling from the tragedy, it was Chris who had seen first that unless action was taken, the farm could soon be facing a crisis. They had even considered 'set-aside', where the entire farm would be abandoned, and all the men sacked, in return for an eighty-pound per acre gift from the Government, but much to everyone's relief, the family ruled this out. The profitability of the hop-gardens now assumed a greater importance than ever.

It also meant some hard-headed decisions about Glade Farm's prize-winning cattle, the herds that had meant so much to Sara, and which she and Tony had worked so hard to develop.

'Some of the cattle are going to have to go,' said Tony, swigging his beer. 'In fact, quite a lot are going to have to go.'

'All of them are going to have to go,' said Chris.

'Except the Dexters.'

'We'll probably keep some of the Dexters in Sara's memory, but the Belties will have to go, and in all we might have to lose about a hundred cattle, which is sad, very sad. Death duties, bank charges, overheads, it's one of those things.'

'You've got to analyse each enterprise and question its viability,' said Chris, using slightly different terminology from his father's. 'If it's not pulling its weight, it's got to go. We're going to have to avoid making emotional decisions.'

It was on the narrow, winding lane to Farringdon, just after the Bonners and Patrick Hodson had shot past her on their bicycles, waving, and had sped quickly out of sight, that Hilda struck disaster.

The muscles of the upper part of both legs, unused to such strenuous and prolonged periods of activity, were suddenly all gripped by a fierce cramp. Both legs seized up simultaneously and, paralysed by the spasm and unable to pedal, Hilda had found herself being catapulted through the air and deposited, rather ignominiously, in a large bed of nettles on the verge.

Fortunately, nobody appeared to have witnessed this extraordinary display of gymnastics, so Hilda just sat, stunned, unable to move, and hoped that the pain would gradually start to ebb away, while the nettles wrought a terrible revenge upon her lower legs and arms.

It was indeed a blow; but of one thing, Hilda was quite determined. The temptation to telephone her sister for help and transport back must be resisted at all costs.

=== **FOURTEEN** ===

'Well, am I glad to see you!' said Margaret, as her sister hauled up the bike, and leant it against the wall of the cottage. Hilda looked exhausted, but triumphant. 'I'd heard from Linda that you were on the way, so I rushed home and turned on the water so you can have a good hot bath. The bubbles are nearly up to the ceiling!'

'How wonderful,' said Hilda.

After sitting in the nettles beside the lonely road from East Tistead for over half-an-hour, Hilda's thigh muscles had seemed at last to have embarked on the long, painful journey back to normality, so rather gingerly she heaved herself up, and hobbled over to the bicycle, still lying, where it had thrown her, a few yards away on the side of the verge.

Reluctantly, she'd decided to skip the ominously steep climb up to Selborne and Newton Valence, and had aimed straight for home, back up the main road, but even so, she had managed no less than twenty-one churches, and raised one hundred and twelve pounds.

'Cath Bonner's done all thirty-three,' said Margaret.

'I'm not surprised.'

Margaret had been fed with a series of reports about Hilda's dramatic piece of gymnastics from incoming cyclists who'd passed her sister on the way back, and she was rather proud, and certainly relieved, to see Hilda back safely.

'I think it's jolly good, what you've done, jolly good, for, er, for you – '

'You were going to say, for an old lady!'

'For an old 'un! I think it's jolly good. Jolly good!'

Everyone had to admit there was an awful irony in the news from the Village Stores, so soon after its fiftieth anniversary celebrations.

Tony Holmes, now throwing himself into his official duties as chairman of the Parish Council, summoned Eric Hale, the clerk, for an emergency meeting. The shop was losing trade, and if it were forced to close, it would be a heavy blow for the village: with it would go the Post Office, the hairdressing salon, Terry's vital delivery round to customers like Edy Parrot and Ma Cox, and, some would say, the heart of the community.

'It's going to be a battle,' said Tony. 'Seventy-five to twenty-five that it closes, Eric?'

'It's the only village shop within miles. All the others in this part of Hampshire, Froyle, Blacknest, Binsted, they've all gone, over the last two or three years.'

'How much trade is Alan losing?'

'He estimates that it's dropped by about twenty-five

per cent because of the parking problem. There's some urgency, Tony. It would be a disaster if it went.'

'Can't let it go.'

Over the years, the Village Stores had become a victim of the very main road which had spawned its existence back in the forties. With a rumbling convoy of lorries and cars speeding past just a few feet from the shop's door all day, every day, there was nowhere for customers to park, since the shop had sold the land used earlier for parking. In the past the problem had been solved by parking in the forecourt of the Star close by. But this was of course dependent on the goodwill of the landlord, and arrangements had to be made with the new incumbent at the Star. Mr Cooper is a man of military stature, background and attitude, who disapproved of the cavalier way villagers assumed they had a God-given right to use his parking area, with the result that many of Alan's customers drove to shop in Alton or Farnham instead, and his takings plummeted.

Tony and Eric Hale drew up their battle-plan. A way might be found to subsidise Mr Wheatley's enterprise, either by adding a few pennies to everybody's community charge, or by invoking a little-known Government pledge revealed by some thorough research of Hansard by Mr Hale, by which district councils could be made to waive the business rates of vital village stores and Post Offices, to enable them to survive.

After his meeting with Eric Hale, Tony trudged off down to Bury Court, on a mission he'd been dreading for some days.

He had always assumed that Sara's Beltie herd would be sold off piecemeal over the next year, but then he'd had a timely call from Her Majesty's Prison

Department. They wanted to buy the entire herd, there and then, and offered Tony as near as dammit the five hundred pounds per beast he'd been hoping for. The deal was as good as done.

'At first, when they said HM Prisons, I thought it was a joke,' said Tony, 'But no, quite serious. They want to send them to the prison at Rugby, which would have amused Sara no end, the thought of her cattle being looked after by the criminal fraternity.

'It was a very hard decision. I look at all those cattle, and I think Sara bought all those, and went all over to get them; and here am I, saying, go. It's very sad. I shall be very sorry to see them go, I shall miss them.

'But they will still be known as the Carlton herd, after Sara's second name, the name won't be altered. They'll go to all the shows, they'll go to the Royal, so if one does well, it may be one of Sara's cattle that bred it, so she'll still be remembered.'

Now, in what he said was one of the saddest days of his life, Tony had to break some bad news to Sara's cattleman, Bob Bates, who'd been brought up in the village, and had married, years ago, the sister of one of Tony's farmhands from Isington. He had worked with cattle all his life. There was no option but to make Bob redundant.

On the other side of the main road, in the kitchen of his cottage by Bentley Green Farm, another of Tony's men, Jim Harden, just couldn't stop hugging his daughter Cherie. She'd been driven home from Heathrow by her mother, after the trip to Maryland.

'You look great, Cher!' said Jim, his still blotchy

face split by an enormous grin. He knew immediately from her pretty, sparkling face, that the trip had been anything but harrowing.

It turned out that Cherie had met a college boy, Phil, who'd been in charge of the pool at the complex.

'She didn't want to come home,' said her mother. 'He took a real shine to her. When they said to her, right, you can come back in two months time, she said, oh no! all because of Phil. She was hoping they'd say two weeks. She loves it!'

The money was still pouring in, Jim said. Sponsored roller-skating, car boot sales, airline tickets from people they'd never met. Things were looking good.

'What were the staff like?'

'They were wonderful, unbelievable. They took us out for trips, to theme parks, to the theatre, it was great. You think they're doing you a favour – but they think you're doing them one! Because we're English, they just love the accent. They spent the whole time making Cherie and me talk. Even the doctors asked us out to dinner. I went out with a doctor and his wife – Cherie didn't come because she was out gallivanting with Phil!'

'Got his telephone number?' asked Jim. Cherie nodded. 'Give him a ring next time.'

'First thing on the agenda, I think.'

The three of them, father, mother and daughter, sat around the table, drinking coffee and laughing, just like old times.

It was always a scramble to get the gardens at Jenkyn Place ready for opening to the public at the beginning of April.

The mild winter had much to answer for. The daffodil and hyacinth bulbs were already on the wane, and Stuart Hume, the head gardener, had had the great lawns which had grown long and shaggy over innumerable frostless days cut three times. The big white flowers of the Christmas Rose had been outstanding; the roses were sprouting, and already there was a little colour on the blossom of the apple and crab apple trees dotted throughout the gardens, a remnant of the war years when, unlike today, food production was paramount, and the orchards and vegetable plots had ruled supreme.

The biggest task was staking the thousands of perennials, particularly the taller plants like the delphiniums, in the two great herbaceous borders that young Walter Sherfield had helped create in the 1930s, and which explode into a divided sea of colour in June and July. For Stuart and his two men, it's a job which takes weeks to complete, but to the specialist their efforts are worth every moment; today the borders are considered amongst the finest in the country.

'It's such an exciting time of year,' says Mrs Coke. 'And I do so love visitors to come and see everything we've done. In the old days, it was rather sad, there'd be beautiful, beautiful flowers everywhere and nobody there to see them.'

They had opened the gardens in the late forties for sixpence a head, and each year the number of visitors grew, until now ten thousand people a year visit Jenkyn Place, and Mrs Coke has had to make a car park in the old field beside John O'Pease Cottage on the other side of Hole Lane. The gardens have become a charitable trust, so all the money raised goes back into the soil, just as Gerald Coke had intended when the trust was formed, a few months before his death.

Already this year, Mrs Coke had confirmed bookings for several coachloads of enthusiasts including, much to her delight, parties from France, Holland, and, most unusually, from New York. Old Walter Sherfield and Jessie were on stand-by to man the gate, and in her brighter moments, with the sun at last brushing aside the days of the endless grey, Mrs Coke decided that perhaps this might turn out to be a brilliant summer, after all.

FIFTEEN

After years of contented stability, when each new season seemed almost indistinguishable from the last, and events merged seamlessly into one another, everything was now changing in Tony Holmes' world.

Of course, there had been the trauma of the last twelve months, but the repercussions seemed unending. The Belties had gone to Rugby, and Bob Bates was looking around for work. Chris had suggested that to raise capital, the farm down at Isington, near Monty's old house, which had remained almost unchanged since Tony was a boy, should be sold, or developed into industrial units. The Village Stores was in trouble too.

Now came the news that Bentley had been awaiting for half a century. The County Council had finally agreed to allocate the six million pounds required to build the bypass, and the village was bracing itself for the fastest and most dramatic change in its history.

Tony had organised a public meeting in the War Memorial Hall, and the consensus of the villagers favoured the Yellow Route, the most southerly of three options put forward, which would throw a great concrete rampart up beyond Meadow House and Rectory Field Cottages, leaving the bulk of the village to the north, and the River Wey and station to the south.

For the Holmes family, it would cause disarray; the new road would run right through four of their large fields, and render two smaller ones useless for cultivation; in short, it would slice the farm into two quite separate parts.

As the locals of the Chequers knew only too well, Tony and Chris were ambivalent about the bypass. On the one hand there was the reality of a development for which the village craved; on the other, the inevitable distruption and division of their land.

Now, too, there were all the minutiae of the project to attend to, more decisions, not about routes now, but about access, slip-roads, bridges, junctions, compensation, noise. The Council had organised a second meeting, a consultation they called it, to convince the villagers the details of the plan were right.

Tony was far from convinced.

'Chris, are you going down to this meeting? There'll probably be some little dogs from the council there, who'll jump up and down, and bark, if you dare cross their path.'

'One of us had better go. It is going right through our land, after all, which is a bit of a bloody nuisance.'

'Bloody nuisance.'

Like many farmers, Tony and Chris hold an instinctive distrust of governmental authority, particularly when it manifests itself as little men in grey suits waving pointers over the maps of their land.

'Seems absolutely ludicrous that they're spending

£50,000 on this consultation, it would be better spent on the bypass itself. We've only been waiting fifty years for it.'

'Just as long as the village turns up, and has a go at them. It's got to happen, though, we've got to face facts.'

'I suppose anything's better than what we do now, crossing the A31 ten times a day, and that's a death-trap. And it might turn the village back into being a village again.'

'Providing they do it properly,' said Tony. 'I'm going to go and thrash it out with them.'

With that, he blew his nose on a great red and white spotted handkerchief and set off down to the Hall, with his jaw pushed forward in the kind of obstinately determined way that, to those who knew him well, was a signal, as clear as a beacon, that trouble lay ahead.

It was during the 1950s that the county council approached the Bentley Cricket Club, and told them that the village bypass was going to be built right through the middle of the old cricket pitch by Station Road, and since work was due to start soon, they'd better think about moving it.

Old Walter Sherfield was captain then, just after the year he'd scored one hundred wickets in a season. They had approached Mr Coke at Jenkyn Place, who gave them a field by the school in School Lane. It was drained and cut, and although the bypass wasn't built, the village cricket was moved there, and there it remains today.

Now all the renewed talk of the bypass had

prompted Walter to write about the subject for this
month's '*My Life and Times in Bentley*' column for the
parish magazine.

"Charlie Redford lived over the green at Preston
Cottages," wrote Walter. "He had just one walking
pace. I remember on more than one occasion old
Charlie would come across the footpath on a Saturday
afternoon while cricket was in progress on the old recre-
ation ground. Play had to stop while he walked across,
and he neither looked or spoke to anyone. Alf Raggett
was a good bowler for years."

Jessie came in with a cup of tea, and read over his
shoulder.

'He was a good player, Alf.'

'He had a trial for Surrey,' said Walter. 'But he
couldn't take it up because he had to look after his
mother.'

"As time went on, and Sunday cricket came into
being, our men voted to play Sunday cricket rather
than turn out on Saturdays, so that ended our Saturday
sport, bad luck."

'You didn't agree with that, Walt, did you?'

'I did not. We had a meeting in the Hall, and they
all voted for it. But I couldn't do my cricket, and be sure
to be back at Church in time for bell-ringing. I told 'em,
if you were asked to work on a Sunday, you'd play
merry Hell! They took no notice.'

The present chairman of the village cricket team
was John Dobson, and whilst Walter was putting the
finishing touches to his article, John was switching off
his teletext machine and locking up the modestly-sized
office of the Bentley and Froyle Oil Company. Over the
next few months, he would be spending rather more of
his time than usual at the bar of the Star, which

between spring and autumn became the official headquarters of the village cricketing fraternity.

John had just returned from a visit to Poland, to open up new oil business, and as he set off across the few yards towards the pub, there was a jaunty bounce to his stride.

It was spring; and whether in his office or outside it, that meant days of endless cricket.

There was an unusually quiet air of efficiency inside the War Memorial Hall. Stands carrying huge blown-up maps and plans of Bentley had been placed in an arc around the walls, with thick red lines tracking across them, where the draughtsmen had laboured to illustrate the precise location and dimensions of the by-pass for the people who were to live beside it. The proposed junctions, bridges and slip-roads were marked in blue.

There were three, neat council men, dressed indeed in grey suits and identifiable by large lapel-badges, hovering confidently in front of the plans, smiling at the villagers as they circulated, answering their enquiries in polite but firm, hushed tones, rather like librarians.

Then Tony Holmes arrived.

He marched straight up to the smallest of the grey-suited men, and launched, without any hesitation, into the attack.

'You know the Froyle entrance, down at Froyle Mill?' he demanded.

'I do,' said the council man, rather like a man about to be wrongly accused of murder.

'You're shutting that, aren't you? Yes.'

Alton Road and the War Memorial Hall

'We're shutting the central reservation.'

'And you're altering the other side.'

'We are.'

'Well, why don't you leave that alone?'

The man took a deep breath.

'It was all part of a package of road safety, which – '

'That part of the village couldn't care less! And what about the buses?'

'We received comments that suggested that – '

'Those people who made comments, and I know who they were, have left the village!'

'And I think we've looked at the comments – '

'The people down that end of Froyle are hopping mad about it!'

'One of the aspects is – '

'They say, who's been interfering?'

The council man looked helplessly at his collea-gues, in a silent entreaty for assistance, but it was as

though they, along with everyone else in the room, had become nothing more than a spellbound audience to the spectacle centre stage.

'You can close the central reservation, put plants in it, but for God's sake leave the other bit open, for the buses! Don't waste any more money!'

'They'll get the bus in virtually – '

'The bus stops right outside for them. There are certain things in the country which happen like this. They know the people in the houses, and they stop for them!'

'What we're trying to do is improve – '

'Road safety! I know. Forget that!'

'You can't forget it!'

'But there is no safety on that road. Where's the safety?'

'But if we extend the dual carriageway – '

'You're already extending it!'

'But somebody coming off the by-pass – '

'Keeps coming!'

'Coming this way – '

'Keeps coming!'

'On this section – '

'Yes, Alton to Farnham – '

'May have been able to overtake,' said the council man, for the first time in the exchange able to complete a sentence.

'Where?' growled Tony.

'On that first section.'

'No they wouldn't!'

J ohn Dobson had settled in comfortably at the Star, and was now deep in cricketing conversation with his old friend Albert Wheatley, erstwhile East End evacuee, and one of the founding fathers of the Village Stores dynasty.

'First time I played with Albert, eighteen years ago, I hit the ball and we ran one, and since the ball was still out there, I said come on, Albert, come again! He said, hang on a minute, lad, come here – I only run ones at the moment.'

These days the two men only played once a year, for the traditional fixture between the current Bentley team and the Chairman's Eleven, and it was the details of this event that the two men were ostensibly here to discuss.

They'd been joined by another old-timer, John Perrin.

'I remember knocking on John's door the day he came back from his honeymoon,' said Albert. 'I got Marjorie, his wife, on my side, and he was given instructions to play that Sunday, and he's been playing ever since. That was thirty-five years ago. Marjorie didn't mind a bit.'

'It was probably a relief to get rid of him,' said John Dobson.

'Yes, by that time she'd got into the routine,' said John Perrin. 'She was quite happy to see me go!'

After a spell as captain, John Dobson had given up village cricket in the seventies, when he'd gone to Curaçao in the Caribbean for Shell, and later to the United States. When he came back to town and established the Bentley and Froyle Oil Company, Albert had him elected Chairman in his absence because he couldn't find anyone else to take it on. John had only known he'd become Chairman because he'd seen it in the printed fixture list.

'Are we going to be able to raise a team, Albert?'

'We'll dragoon a few Wheatleys in to help out.'

'Keith available?'

Keith Wheatley, Albert's son, had played for the Hampshire First Eleven in the late sixties, and his presence on the chairman's side could be the perfect guarantee of victory.

'I'll have a word with him.'

'Daren't let him bat for too long, though. I've got to fly to Bulgaria on oil business first thing on the day after the match.'

It was now like a Wimbledon final in the War Memorial Hall, the heads of the growing crowd of people moving in absolute unison as the argument bounced between Tony and the grey-suited council man.

'I think all this is a pure waste of money,' concluded Tony, now towering over his adversary. He's a formidable man even when not aroused, and this suddenly seemed like the perfect vent for the months of anger and frustration.

'Nobody would have been aware of the fact – ' persisted the man, blindly determined to finish his point.

'Another thing. You upset the locals, the country-side is losing enough of its ruddy amenities, now you're knocking the buses. You want to think of these things, you don't think of 'em! What's this costing, anyway?'

'The display? We have a statutory duty – '

'Waste of money! This has been going on, and on, and on, and on! Not an argument, in my language!'

Afterwards, Tony left the man, who was still slightly quivering, and strode out past the crowd. He recognised a face, and smiled.

'How was I?' asked Tony. 'Was I all right?'

The crowd laughed.

As he walked out into the car park, Tony realised he hadn't felt so good for weeks.

SIXTEEN

You can tell when summer begins in Bentley; little wooden signs saying 'Teas At The Church' mysteriously sprout up overnight on the verges and junctions the length of Hole Lane, although it's in the immediate vicinity of Jenkyn Place that the signs can be observed at their most dense.

It's one of Hilda and Margaret's fund-raising ideas, of course, and today looked like being one of the busiest of the whole year. They had been tipped off that a party of American horticultural enthusiasts were due to visit the Jenkyn Place gardens, and all morning they'd been busying about, hammering in extra signs, transporting a conveyor-belt of home-made cakes and biscuits up Hole Lane from the cottage, and finally taking the car right up the cobbled pathway to the church door itself, to unload the vast urn that was required for the tea.

If the weather's good, the sisters take out the tables and chairs from the Sunday School room where they're stacked, and lay them out beneath the great beech in the graveyard, at the back of the church, where there's a captivating view to the east, over the gentle hills which run down towards Farnham.

'Sometimes they sit on the tombstones themselves,' said Margaret. 'We had an old lady of eighty-nine who came and said, I've done so many things in my life, dear, but never had tea in a churchyard before, which delighted her.'

The idea was that the bulk of trade would come from visitors leaving Jenkyn Place, who'd see the barrage of signs, and wander up to the church a few hundred yards away. In previous years, the teas had been on offer only on Sundays, but with the big push now required for the bell-tower restoration work, along with the small army of volunteers who'd responded to the parish magazine appeal, this year they hoped to launch a four-days-a-week service.

The funds were badly needed. As predicted, the builders had found plenty more work that needed doing, as builders will; as well as being ravaged by the beetle, many of the timbers in the roof of the bell tower were rotten. For years, water had been penetrating the lead, where it had stretched and shrunk around the nails, and much of this too now needed replacing. Another £13,000 had to be spent on the stonework in the east window, which was found to be crumbling, and the work on the old organ, which everyone hoped might start soon, was likely to be postponed. But however depressing this news, none of it was likely to dent the sisters' determination to raise as much as they could from the teas.

'We've had twenty-four offers from people who'll make cakes, or biscuits, or scones, and I'm hoping some of the Guides will help serve. We've even had people who've come for tea, and then helped with the washing up when they see we're busy!'

Today they had produced a splendid range of biscuits: hundreds of lemon, cherry, fruit and ginger biscuits, all baked in the oven at home.

'It's surprising how quickly they go,' said Hilda. 'How many people do you think we're going to get today, Margaret?'

'I've got enough cups to do fifty at a time, we should get at least that, although with these Americans here, we could get anything up to two hundred!'

Curiously, the news that the bypass was at last going to get underway helped solve another of the village's most pressing problems, and in a way no one had predicted.

For years, developers had been applying relentless pressure for planning permission to build on land between the main road and Babs Field. The parish council had objected, not least on the grounds that the new traffic generated by the estate could only make the crossroads by the War Memorial Hall more murderous still. It had eventually been agreed that building would start only when the council had made a definite commitment to begin work on the new road.

With this now in hand, the bulldozers wasted no time in moving in, and soon the skeletons of thirty-six houses started to rise from the ground, most of them of the larger, executive-style so ridiculed by the old-timers, but some of them at least, on the insistence of Tony Holmes and the parish council, one-bedroomed starter homes.

'Why shouldn't the younger people stay in the

village?' he argued. 'Why should they be forced out when they were born in the place? This village will disappear without the young people.'

For Albert's nephew Alan Wheatley, now in charge of the Village Stores, the development brought with it an unexpected and timely bonus. For the next twelve months, there'd be fifty workmen labouring on the site – fifty hungry workmen, fifty empty bellies, always anxious to buy sandwiches, crisps, drinks, and newspapers from a handy village shop. Suddenly the spectre of hundreds of navvies descending on the village to spend years building a bypass didn't seem so awesome, after all; not to Alan Wheatley, anyway.

Furthermore, Mr Cooper from the Star had now become more accommodating: he had agreed that, after all, villagers could use the Star car-park at any time of the day, except between the hours of 11 a.m. and 3 p.m., when his passing lunch trade was to have priority. Everyone agreed that this was a very fair and reasonable solution. Mr Cooper, or Trevor as he had now become known, even endeared himself to Hilda and Margaret by raising eighty pounds over the bar towards the bell-tower restoration fund.

Trevor had also been revealed as a very creditable medium pace bowler, so he was immediately snapped up by John Dobson and Albert Wheatley, desperate to bolster the previously unspectacular bowling attack of the Chairman's Eleven for the forthcoming match. With Trevor's help, they had almost managed to scrape a full side together.

'I've got rather a lot of Wheatleys on my team,' said John Dobson, quite unabashed. There was Albert Wheatley, of course, and Keith Wheatley, the former Hampshire player. They'd been joined by David

Wheatley, who is Albert's other son, and Dennis Wheatley, a cousin. To build up the team, John had press-ganged some of his oil colleagues into service: Daniel, another former Shell man, his solicitor Les, and Chris, whom he'd worked with in the States. Jonathan Morris, a handsome stroke-player who sometimes plays for an MCC side, the son of the legendary Mrs Morris from the village school, had agreed to play; and then there was Trevor.

'Apart from Jonathan not one of us is under forty-five,' said John.

'Don't worry about that,' said Albert. 'The combined age of cover and extra cover last time was one hundred and thirty.'

Now that the teams were organised, another pre-match meeting at the Star was deemed essential, to discuss tactics.

'We'll have to bat first whatever the toss, because Trevor has to close the pub at three thirty, and we need to use him as a bowler,' said John, scribbling officiously on a scrap of paper. 'Once Trevor's done his bowling stint, we'll send him back up here so he's all ready with drinks lined up for when we finish, which must be by opening time. Seven o'clock, Trevor?'

'Seven, skipper.'

John then cleared his throat, rapped his empty glass on the bar, and addressed his troops.

'Right then boys, Albert will open, because he's the oldest man in the team by quite a long way, along with Jonathan Morris, who's the youngest. Just watch your running between wickets – you two have a nasty habit of ending up in the same place at the same time.'

'Good afternoon, ladies and gentlemen,' said Mrs Coke, as loudly as she could, and the large group of Americans who'd just climbed off the coach quietened slightly to hear her.

'Come this way, if you please. Guides and postcards are available over here. Would you all like to follow me?'

Mrs Coke set off at a cracking pace, through a little oak gate off the drive, and into the enchanting walled Dutch garden, leaving a slightly flustered Walter Sherfield to cope with current exchange rates between the dollar and the pound.

The visitors were all members of the distinguished Brooklyn Horticultural Society of New York, and were immediately impressed by what they saw.

'Too bad you don't have a camera, ain't it?' said one lady to her companion, sounding for all the world like Scarlett O'Hara.

'Ain't that pretty, ain't that beautiful beside the other flowers?'

'It's a tree peony, looks like Suffruticosa, they stay woody at the bottom, they don't die back down to the ground, like the others,' her companion replied.

'He has a doctorate in botany. He likes plants, he doesn't like gardens!' said the woman, to those behind.

'I enjoy the gardens, but I'm just as interested in the little things growing along the roadside. I wish I could stop the bus every few miles, and get out.'

'You're just impossible! Oh, my, this is a neat one, ain't it?' she said, moving close to admire Suffruticosa once more.

'It's magnificent. I don't think I've ever seen this white one before, it's just a beauty!'

Up at the church, preparations for the impending American onslaught were well in hand. The cakes and different coloured biscuits were laid out in serried little rows, and the giant urn was coming to the boil.

'I think Americans might find it rather fun to have tea in a church,' said Margaret. 'The difficult moment is when they're still pouring through the door, and we haven't finished washing up, and the tables are full – that's the nerve-racking moment.'

'We've had queues half way down the church.'

'Are we quite ready now?'

'Water's boiling, milk and sugar's out.'

The minutes ticked by.

'They haven't really had very long to look around the garden,' said Hilda at length, breaking the silence. 'And if they've come all the way from America, I should think they're very interested.'

'We're ready for them!'

A fair quantity of ale had passed in a one-way direction over the bar of the Star before Trevor called last orders, and the chairman's pre-match tactics talk started to draw to a close.

They had been joined by some of next week's opponents, the regular village players, who had started the season with a run of awesome victories.

Their captain was Paul Ellis, a young and alarmingly muscular electrician.

'I'm quietly confident,' said Paul, downing his pint in one. 'We've got a trick or two up our sleeves.'

'Have you?' asked John, in genuine astonishment. 'Getting us drunk before the game?'

Paul was about to become a father for the first

St. Mary's Church

time. He'd told his wife he'd be home hours ago, but he somehow found himself accepting another pint none the less.

'It's actually due a week on Sunday, but of course it may happen any day now. I'm rather hoping I don't get the call on Match Day.'

'We were only allowed to have our babies in winter,' said John. 'Albert told my wife, you're not to have any children in the cricket season!'

At last Hilda and Margaret heard a solitary pair of footsteps echoing through the empty church, and down through the vestry to the makeshift tea-rooms.

'Ah, here they are at last!'

But the pair were English, and were far from being the vanguard of a huge, thirsty multitude. They were alone.

'How nice to see you,' said Margaret, gamely

hiding her disappointment. 'Have you enjoyed the gardens?'

'Very interesting,' said the couple.

Margaret gave them tea and biscuits, and cheerfully tried to keep a conversation alive, whilst Hilda crept out of the back and set off down the lane at a brisk pace to Jenkyn Place, to find out what on earth had happened to the coachload of American visitors.

'May we ask, how old is that tree out at the front, the yew?'

'Some say it's four hundred years old, some say it's more,' said Margaret. 'It's tremendous, isn't it? There were originally a dozen, but one by one we're losing them.'

'Very interesting. To think we've lived so near, for so long, but never been here before.'

'Where have you come from?' asked Margaret, topping up the cups.

'Farnborough. And we shall certainly come again.'

Just then, Hilda appeared in the doorway, slightly out of breath, grey-faced.

'They've gone.'

Margaret looked up, in disbelief.

'The Americans have gone? Without having tea?'

'Yes, I've just been there to see, and they've driven off!' said Hilda, still not quite able to grasp that they'd got two hundred undrunk cups of tea awaiting disposal.

'What a shame!' said Mrs Bonner, who'd bumped into Hilda in the lane, and had come up to offer moral support.

'After all that!' said Margaret.

'Never mind,' said Hilda, gathering her composure. 'We've got some nice visitors here already, so not to worry.'

The English couple were promptly offered a third cup of tea.

A few minutes later, Mrs Coke arrived.

'Absolutely worn out,' she said, collapsing in a chair.

'Tea?'

'It'll save my life.'

'What happened to the Americans?'

'I don't really know. I think they were worn out, too, quite honestly. They've done a garden this morning, then they went to lunch, then they came to me, and they're staying near Winchester, then they're going out to dinner – how kind, thank you so much!' Mrs Coke took the tea as though she was indeed near to passing away from dehydration.

'Biscuit?'

'Yes please. They were very grand, the Americans. They brought me a magnolia which only the Queen and I now have, I gather, which is very exciting, a lovely yellow magnolia.'

Later Hilda and Margaret washed up their visitors' three cups and saucers.

'It's a bit disappointing, in a way, you sit up here a long time for nothing in particular. But never mind, it's always worth it, if only for a few people,' said Hilda. 'Anyway, we've got all the stuff up here now, and it's all planned, ready for the rest of the season. A splendid dress-rehearsal!'

SEVENTEEN

Most of the serious business at Glade Farm was done over the kitchen table, with the two dogs Esau and Jacob snoring contentedly on their bean-bags, a pot of coffee constantly alive on the cooking range, and down below the big picture window, the little black Dexters, endlessly grazing, day and night.

The subject under debate this morning was the United Nations High Commission for Refugees, not a frequent topic for discussion amongst the Holmes family; at least, not until Pom had decided that for her third-year industrial placement, part of Oxford Poly-technic's Business Studies course, she would offer her services to the UN.

'Most people go to commercial organisations for the year, like IBM or Marks and Spencer, and are probably earning a lot of money,' said Pom, who is darker than her mother was, but whose slim build and mannerisms seem sometimes almost identical. 'I wanted to do something where there'd be some benefit at the end of it, other than just a pay-packet.'

Her philanthropy didn't come as a complete surprise to her family. Pom's a traveller; she had been to Israel, and had walked the famous four-day Milford Trek across the fjords of southern New Zealand; but it was her adventures in Africa, where she'd travelled with twenty other young people in an old army truck from Kenya to the Cameroons, Tanzania and Zaire, that had awoken her mind to the appalling plight of so many refugees across the world. As she frequently points out, according to the UN, no less than seventeen million of them were in desperate need of help.

Pom had spent much of the year with the UN Association at their London office, calling art galleries and contacts in the art world, and writing dozens of letters each week to refugee communities. She had been asked to track down artists in exile who would be prepared to donate pictures to a special exhibition celebrating the fortieth anniversary of the UN Council for Refugees.

The climax to the event was to be an auction of the pictures to raise money for refugees; and Pom and the rest of the team hoped that if nothing else it might help make the British public take more notice of what was happening elsewhere in the world.

It had been very hard work, much harder than she'd expected, and she'd come to relish her visits back to Glade Farm as a chance to recuperate. All that remained now was the auction itself; after that, she'd be back home with Tony for the long summer break.

'How many pictures did you manage to get in the end?' asked Tony, royally holding up his mug for more coffee. Upstairs they could hear the drone of Maureen hard at work with the new vacuum.

'About a hundred and twenty. Many of them are

Eastern European artists, some British, some Kurdish and South American refugees.'

'You back up to London now?'

'This afternoon.'

'You've done well.'

'It's begging, really. You get used to asking, after a time. After a year I've become quite good at it.'

He stood at the door, and saw her off, as he always did.

'Good luck! See you next week!'

It was only on his rather belated return home, after the very fluid pre-match tactics talk up at the Star, that the Bentley village cricket captain, Paul Ellis, discovered to his surprise that his wife was already in labour.

This wasn't supposed to have happened for at least another week; but at least an early birth would almost certainly mean he'd be free to play in the Chairman's Match, so it was with a curious mixture of relief and dread, that Paul calmly sat down and started timing his wife's contractions.

They'd studied the books, of course, and when eventually the contractions were only five minutes apart, Paul telephoned Basingstoke Hospital and, by now rather regretting his enthusiasm for tactics talks at the Star, he drove Denise gingerly to the maternity unit, arriving at the ungodly hour of 4.45 a.m. Being a first child, it took another fourteen hours for little Adam to arrive, only five pounds three and a half ounces, but with a mass of dark hair, and when it was all over, and mother and child were fast asleep, Paul drove slowly home and collapsed, utterly exhausted.

Today, three days later, he had almost recovered, and was now back at Basingstoke, this time to pick them both up and bring them home; and today, in contrast, he was driving quickly. He had no choice. The Chairman's Match was due to start in just over an hour.

Paul had packed his cricket kit before he'd left, so that when the three of them arrived home, to be met by a little group of cheering neighbours and his beaming parents-in-law, all he had to do was kiss everyone goodbye, and grab his bag.

'Oh, he's so lovely!' cried Denise's mother, when she saw the sleeping baby, eyes clamped shut.

'Is he playing in this afternoon's match, then?' asked Denise's father.

'He's twelfth man.'

'Isn't he gorgeous?'

'He's fantastic, incredible,' said Paul, looking around for his cricket sweater.

'What time you going to be back tonight?' asked Denise. 'You going to the pub afterwards?'

'Not too late,' said Denise's mother, quietly.

'Not too late, love. Back in time to see His Lordship.'

Before he left, he couldn't resist one last look at his new son.

'I think he might well be opening bat for England one day,' said Paul.

'He's got that look about him.'

'Hasn't he!'

Just as Paul was saying goodbye to his newly-enlarged family, John Dobson was buying a large round of drinks for his players at the Star, and peering out at the torrential rain falling outside. It was so wet that the traffic had even slowed on the main road, although lorries were still throwing up great waves of water so that the front windows of the pub never stopped rattling.

'No hurry to start,' said Albert Wheatley.

'Paul isn't here anyway. Is he going to make it?'

'He said he'd be here, no problem,'

'Not like Paul to be late for a game.'

'Was it a boy or a girl?'

After finishing lunch and rapidly sinking another pint, the rain seemed to ease slightly, and a pitch inspection was declared.

'We've played in worse,' said Albert, as they squelched over to the square.

'Have we got sawdust?'

'The stump-holes have nearly filled up with water,' said John.

'Very high water table here, or at least it used to be,' said Albert. 'And of course it's clay.'

'Do you remember that charity match, Albert, in nineteen-seventy – '

'Seventy-four – ' said Albert.

'Seventy-four, that's it, the pavilion was just foundations, and it rained like hell, and we put two blankets over the wickets, and used the roller on them, to soak it up, and it was still pouring, and my wife said, you guys are completely round the bend.'

'Made a lot of money,' said Albert.

'The wind is swinging round!'

'If we get that weather, from the west, we'll be all right!'

'But it's blowing from the east!'

'It's only when there's puddles on a length, and you just can't get the ball up the other end, that you don't actually play.'

'I would suggest a quarter to three start,' said Albert.

'Agreed.'

So with heavy hearts, they trooped back to the Star, occasionally looking up into the grey skies above, and wearily shaking their heads.

'It's pretty desperate,' said John, waving at Trevor to refill their glasses. 'Not the first time it's happened, nor the last.'

At last Paul arrived, slightly flustered, and very thirsty.

'There's sunshine over Alton way!'

'Don't say that!'

'Congratulations!' said Mrs Morris, who of course had taught Paul's wife years ago, like most of the rest of the village side. 'How's the baby!'

'Very well, very well indeed,' said Paul, sheepishly.

'Delighted you managed to get here!' said John. 'What are you drinking?'

'Six X.'

'To Adam!' said Mrs Morris.

'Look out for Eve!'

'Congratulations, Paul. And to your wife. She went through the hard bit.'

'Oh yes. Cheers!'

'She let you out, then.'

Even though the sun had just appeared, the two teams felt that the honourable course was to stay on a while more at the Star, to wet the baby's head and give his father a memorable launch into fatherhood, so it was considerably after a quarter to three that John Dobson reluctantly ordered his players to down glasses, and prepare for battle. The pitch was now beginning to dry out, and he'd never felt more like scoring a century in his life.

There weren't as many people at the auction as Pom and the others had hoped, although they certainly gave an impression of wealth, as they glided around the room sipping glasses of wine and popping canapés away, hovering every now and then to scrutinise a picture or piece of sculpture.

Pom had spent the last few days rushing around London from one traffic jam to another, collecting the pictures from the various artists who'd offered them, and arranging with Lubinka and Felix to display them to their best around the room. If they sold them all for the prices suggested by the artists, they could raise over fifty thousand pounds.

Pom was stationed on the desk by the main entrance, greeting the guests as they arrived.

'Would you like to fill out a bidding form, sir? If you put your name here, and your address, I'll give you a number, and when your bid comes up, you just wave it in the air. Do you know what you're bidding for?'

'I'd like some of the sculptures.'

'Naomi Blake?'

'There's one by a chap called Rubinstein, *Cat On A Table* I like, also *Head Of A Punk* by Elena Mironova.'

'Right, good.'

'How's it going?' asked Felix.

'Not too bad.'

'You're looking a bit whacked, Pom.'

'I am, I'm exhausted.'

The auctioneer was motioning people to take a seat.

'This exhibition lasts until Saturday,' he announced, and gradually a hush fell over the room. 'So you will be able to collect your bids from here after 4 p.m. on Saturday afternoon.' He cleared his throat, a little apprehensively. 'There are plenty of empty seats here at the front, so don't be afraid to come forward, please.'

'Unfortunately Lots One A and One B are withdrawn, so we start with Lot Two, the Guillermo Laarcon sculpture, and I'll start here at four hundred pounds . . . four hundred pounds, ladies and gentlemen . . .'

Not a sound, nor a movement, came from the audience.

'Come along, ladies and gentlemen . . . four hundred pounds . . . don't be afraid to bid! . . . No takers then.

'Lots Three and Four are withdrawn, so we come to Lot Five *Assault*, which I'll start at one hundred and ten pounds . . .'

Pom stood in the darkness at the back of the auction-room, her job now over, and watched with a sinking heart as one by one the lots failed to make the figures they'd all so hoped for.

'Lot Fifty! Do I hear seventy pounds? Seventy pounds, ladies and gentlemen!' There was a faint note of desperation in the auctioneer's voice. 'Sixty pounds then! Sixty pounds, ladies and gentlemen . . .'

'A lot of the people here just aren't bidding,' said Pom. 'A lot of them are the artists who've come to watch their work being sold, which isn't much use, although it's good to see them supporting us. So many of them have been very enthusiastic, and so glad they were able to help in some way.'

Pom was warming to a theme which had been

growing stronger in her mind, especially over the last three months of frantic activity to get the auction ready in time.

'I'm sure a lot of people do want to help, but unless an opportunity like this comes along, people don't really know what to do. You look at pictures of refugees on television and in the newspapers, and it really makes you want to do something.'

It was as though the auctioneer, at that moment, was echoing Pom's precise sentiment.

'I'd like to remind those of you who are saving your bids for later on,' said the auctioneer, 'Not only to remember that everything you give will be going to a very worthwhile cause, but that you'll end up with a tangible work of art as well. It's very well worth bidding. Now, Lot Fifty-eight, Simon Gooch, *In The Ruins Of Spitak*. Do I hear thirty-five pounds . . . thirty pounds . . .'

'It's up to them now,' said Pom. 'It's up to them to buy. It doesn't really matter any more. I've done what I can.'

EIGHTEEN

Whether it was as a result of the prolonged cele-brations, the trauma of becoming a father, or the effect of blinding sun on a damp, steaming pitch, no-one will ever be sure, but the sad truth was that Paul Ellis, captain of the Bentley team, was out for a Golden Duck, bowled first ball by a stunning delivery from Mrs Morris' son, Jonathan.

'It was well pitched up, and I just played down the wrong line,' said a slightly bemused Paul afterwards. 'I saw it leave the bowler's hand, and I saw it hit the wicket.'

'Hard luck, Paul,' said Mr Morris, who'd missed the action. 'Who got you out?'

'Your son did!'

'Oh Lord, good, I'm sorry about that, rather mixed feelings!'

'It was a good ball.'

'It wasn't that you wanted to get out quickly so you can go home to Denise?'

'No, I just needed a beer.'

Out on the boundary, old Walter watched with approval as the Bentley side, despite their early loss, began to build up a sound start to the innings.

'This kind of pitch is so wet, you only get ones or fours,' said Walter. 'I remember when I got seventy-five runs against an army team from Bordon one year. Hit a six, right out of the ground, over the stile, over Station Road, right into the field next door. Two balls later, had another slog, clean bowled.

'One year, back in the forties, we played a team from Charterhouse School, which included young Peter May, who later became the great Peter May, captain of England, and chairman of the selectors. The Charterhouse boys used to like coming to Bentley 'cos old Captain Eggar, an old Charterhouse man himself, always gave 'em a great spread of strawberries and cream. We didn't let young May get away with much though. I was a fast right-armer at the time, and it was either me or old Alf Raggett who clean bowls him, I can't remember which of us now, but we lived off that story for quite a few years.'

After tea, which was really a euphemism for more beer, Albert Wheatley opened the batting for the Chairman's Eleven, with Jonathan Morris at the other end. Albert soon received what he later claimed to be the best ball ever bowled by anybody in the world, and promptly departed. Jonathan, the only regular player in the side, got off to a cracking start, and was soon in double figures. John Dobson joined Jonathan after Albert's departure. Slightly to everyone's surprise, particularly his own, John also started scoring freely, even though, like the rest of his team, he hadn't played a game of cricket since the Chairman's Match last year.

The runs kept coming, and even to old Walter,

who had been watching cricket in the village for over seventy years, this was beginning to look like an innings that would be remembered.

'How much money did you make in the end?' asked Tony, with Pom now home at last from London, for the summer, and he more pleased than ever to see her back. Glade Farm was noisy again, and he was glad of it, with Pom here, and now Fogs too, during the school holidays. Even young Catherine was up there most mornings, when Maureen couldn't find anything else to do with her.

It was the showing season, of course, and in so many previous years, Tony and Sara would have spent much of June and July on the road, sometimes with their little white caravan behind the Range Rover, like rich, happy gypsies, following their cattle-trucks racing up and down the motorways, collecting medals and cups by the sackful.

'Ten thousand pounds,' said Pom.

'How much were you expecting?'

'At one stage we were hoping for as much as fifty thousand.'

'Well, ten thousand is ten thousand more than you had to start with.'

'It is virtually all profit. But I think people have had enough of charity events like this. There's a recession, nobody's buying art any more. It's a pity really, because while there's the danger of overkill, when people have seen enough of starving babies, they don't carry on giving and giving. But with events like the auction, they give, and get something back. If you buy a picture, you've got something you can keep for ever, something to show for it, and every time you look at it, it'll remind you why you bought it.'

'You've still done well.'

'It was important for me to do it. When I started I wanted to do something that would benefit other people as well as me. It's been a good year, and I've done some good work, and gained some valuable experience. It's what I want to do, at the end, when I get my Business Studies degree.'

'What exactly do you want to do?'

'Maybe work for the UN, with refugees, and children. I've decided I'm not greatly motivated by money. There's not much point getting a job that pays thousands of pounds if you don't actually enjoy it.'

'Fair enough.'

'I've spoken to a lot of people over this exhibition, a lot of refugees, and I've tried to imagine what it must be like, leaving everything behind, your family, your friends, your house, and all your belongings, and come to a strange country, not speak the language, and not even have a community to support you.

'There are so many problems in the world, and they're not going to go away, so we've got to try to help.'

'That's all very well, but do you think you really can help?' asked Tony.

Pom thought for a moment.

'I don't know. But I can try. There's no point in sitting back and saying, this is the way the world is. Nobody achieves anything doing that. If you want to do a bit of good, you have to get up, and do something about it.'

At the other end of Hole Lane, a small army of ladies had swept into the War Memorial Hall, and for a few minutes the old walls of the building resounded to the echo of trestle-tables being swiftly erected, and chairs being scraped into position.

These were the ladies of the Flower Show committee, whose proud boast was that the Flower Show had been established long before the loud games and competitions of the Fête had been deemed a necessary adjunct. In their eyes the sanctity of the old marquee, where the flowers and vegetables were displayed, was supreme, and all that went on outside it a mere sideshow.

This was registration day for growers, for the Show was only a week or two away, and a well-oiled operation it was, too.

'Hello Jack, first in, as always,' said Miss Deane, the committee secretary, as old Jack Wiltshire tapped his cap, and sat down to receive his numbered ticket.

A small queue soon formed, and at the end of the line Margaret Evans had already set up shop selling raffle tickets to those awaiting their turn.

'Hello, come and sit down,' said Miss Deane, to a young, dark woman whose bright face she didn't recognise.

'Hello, I'm Christine.'

'Have you entered before?'

'No, this is my first year. We've just moved into a house across the road, at Babs Field.'

'Oh good! That's splendid. Now we give you a number, here it is, thirty-five, and you keep hold of that. It might look complicated, but its a good system, and it's been working well for years.' Miss Deane leant forward a little. 'It was worked out by a General.'

'A General?' said Christine.

'The Show Committee president, Lieutenant-General Sir William Pike. That's why it works so well. Never have any problems with the numbering.'

'We moved to Bentley in February, and we've got to know so many people in the village,' said Christine. 'The Show seems to be quite a village event, doesn't it?'

'Oh yes,' said Miss Deane. 'Particularly the Flower Show.'

'And we want to be part of the village, so we thought we'd enter.'

Christine had recently returned to England with her twin five-year-old boy and girl after an unhappy marriage, and unhappy life, which had ended with a failed business venture in Zimbabwe. Her arrival in Bentley had seemed like the start of a new era, and she was determined to pursue it with vigour.

'My son's got some violas which he's very proud of. He's only five, so can he do it on my entry?'

'Oh, we ought to make a special feature of that, the judges like children entering,' said Miss Deane.

'He didn't really want to enter the children's category, he's so proud of his violas – '

'Oh! He can enter with the grown-ups, you know, on his own if he wants, but we just need to make a note of it.'

'Can he? Oh, he'd love that. Thank you.'

Albert Wheatley, still complaining of his bad luck, was buried in a deckchair and now rather enjoying the arduous job of keeping the score.

'Well played Jonathan!' he muttered, putting down another four. 'No wonder he's doing so well, he's using my old bat.'

Then suddenly the great Jonathan Morris was given out, by an umpire still clad in gumboots, caught behind for fifty-two. All eyes were now on John Dobson, bulging-eyed and beetroot-faced from his unaccustomed exertions, but with a steely look of grim determination fixed on his puffing features. It was as if all those days of watching the England team face disaster time after time on his television set in his office at the Bentley and Froyle Oil Company had prepared him for this very moment; as if he was out in the middle at Lord's itself, one man batting to save the nation from disgrace.

The ball came skidding off the grass, a short ball, and he cut it confidently through covers, and ran like blazes. He made the crease easily, and turned; should they go for a second? At the other end, Keith Wheatley was holding his hand high in the air, pausing.

On the boundary, old Walter shook his head; ones and fours only.

'Yes, come on!' shouted John, and as he set off he suddenly felt a searing pain in the top of his leg, as though the muscles there had spontaneously burst into flame.

Gasping for breath, he stumbled, losing his balance, and desperately tried to stop himself falling.

NINETEEN

'I've written to Peter Tuntuwa, and told him I'll definitely be able to make a quick stop to see them,' said Hilda, handing Margaret a cup of tea, and tickling Fergus the West Highland terrier under his chin.

'So that's definite.'

'That's definite. Malawi Railways have confirmed that the *Ilala* will be back in service by the end of next week.'

For years, Hilda had dreamed of returning to the country that had made such a powerful and indelible impression on her. Recently, she'd had a growing sense that, at seventy-two, if she didn't go back now, she never would. She had toyed with the idea last year, but fears over the Gulf War and its repercussions had made her back down. This time, there seemed nothing in her way, and if she had been hesitating slightly, it was probably nothing more than a momentary lack of courage.

There was no backing down now, anyway, not after she'd sent the letter. The ticket was booked, and already Hilda had started a course of anti-malaria pills.

It was in 1950 that the young Hilda Evans had accepted the offer from an Anglican missionary society of a teaching post in the then British Protectorate of Nyasaland, a small landlocked country largely bordered by Mozambique and Rhodesia, and which, thanks to its lack of strategic importance, natural resources or a seaport, had been allowed to remain virtually undisturbed by the Great Powers since its colonisation at the turn of the century.

It had indeed been a great adventure in Hilda's life. Likoma Island, which lies in the middle of Lake Malawi, the giant lake that makes up almost half the country's geographical area, was a dry, barren little place, dominated by ancient baobab trees, where only the long-suffering cassava crop was tough enough to thrive. The island was totally dependent for supplies on the lake steamer, the *Ilala*, which at that time called in once a month, bearing mountains of food and sacks of mail.

There she had worked tirelessly for nine years, based at the village school built beside the great African cathedral of St Peter's which the early missionaries had built on a site where witches had been burnt, rising up like some incongruous temple to European enterprise in the midst of an African wilderness. She was in charge of seven small schools on Likoma and its tiny neighbouring island, Chizu-mulu. Her pupils were the children of the fishermen, who toiled away with their nets from dawn to dusk amongst the crocodiles in nothing more than dug-out canoes, sending back boxes of the sweetly-flavoured Chambo fish on the *Ilala* for sale at Mzuzu market; and good pupils they were, too. Such was the zeal of the missionaries that at one time, Likoma could claim to be the only settlement in Africa with a one hundred per cent literacy rate amongst its inhabitants.

Of course, there had been little else to do but work. The only European visitors were the scientists who came to study the fish that make the lake one of the world's most valuable wildlife parks. On one occasion Hilda was able to visit the extraordinary hilltop mission station of Livingstonia, created in memory of the first European to discover the lake, in 1859, Dr David Livingstone. Otherwise, she passed the evening hours admiring the sensational sunsets behind the distant mountains, and writing long letters home to Margaret.

Now at last she was returning to Malawi, and during her trip she would be able to make a brief stop at Likoma when the lake steamer called there. Those who knew her well around the village remarked that the prospect of the journey was clearly doing her good, since it sent the colour to her cheeks, and lent an urgency and excitement to her conversation.

'There's a pull about the place, you see, a pull from Africa,' she said. 'It's difficult to get it out of your system.'

'I was only out there for six weeks,' said Margaret. 'On a visit to Hilda. Yet even after only six weeks, I knew that pull and I'd have jumped at the chance of going back. Is Peter Tuntuwa the Dean of the Cathedral?'

Hilda nodded.

'He'll be looking a bit older, I dare say, but then I suppose I am, too.'

'And your God-daughter, Patricia, is she still on the island?'

'I'm not sure, Margaret. But I'll soon be finding out.'

'And I'll be left holding the fort, looking after Fergus.'

John Dobson sat, one leg resting delicately on a cushion, sheets of faxes all over the floor, making a telephone call to Singapore.

'Bloody stupid thing to do, but then it's easy to forget that you're not a young man any more,' he said to his opposite number on the other side of the world, and heard guffaws of laughter in return. 'Should never have gone for that second, but once Jonathan was out, I thought I'd stay to the end and see it through!'

His injury, although extremely painful, had turned out to be nothing more serious than a pulled hamstring. The story of how John Dobson had selflessly disregarded his own safety and steered the Bentley Chairman's Eleven to ultimate victory, had caused much amusement amongst his colleagues in the oil fraternity.

He had to admit it had been something of a triumph. When they'd seen him staggering off the pitch, Mrs Morris had rushed over with a chair and his daughter had thrust a beer in his hand. Eventually he retired home for a hot bath, leaving the rest of the side to take the brilliant opening partnership on to a score of 142, and the first-ever win by a Chairman's Eleven.

Now he'd have to take life a little easier. The injury was taking much longer to heal than it would have done twenty years ago, so it was just as well that his trip to Bulgaria had been postponed. Unfortunately, it wasn't so bad that he was able to cancel another trip, a bit nearer home, which he'd been secretly dreading ever since his birthday.

'I made this throwaway remark earlier in the year,' said John, a rueful expression clouding his face. 'I said I quite fancied going up in a hot-air balloon sometime. I didn't think any more about it. My family, who are always looking for new ideas for birthdays, bought me a trip, and it's due to take off tomorrow.

'Last week I had a trip to Paris, and I decided to go up the Eiffel Tower. I only made it half-way up. I got very nervous, too scared to go up to the top, so now I don't know whether the balloon trip is such a good idea. If the weather's good I shall have to go, because I can't funk out of it now, but to be honest I'm not so sure I want the weather to be good.'

There was an increasing number of hot-air balloons to be seen in the early mornings and evenings over the village, exploiting the thermals created by the valley and the hills either side. They got very short shrift, too, if they happened to land on any of the fields at Glade Farm.

'In the old days we might only see one every six months,' said Tony. 'But now, especially at weekends, they're all over the ruddy place, whooshing the cattle with their burners, and flattening the corn. Cheeky devils!'

Once Chris had had an acrimonious exchange with a pilot, who handed him a pen and map, and asked him to point out the no-go areas around Bentley. Chris had simply drawn a huge circle all round the village.

'Getting all the gear out of the field causes trouble, too,' said Tony. 'They just want to drive in and pick it up, but we make 'em carry it all out. If they ever landed on my hop-gardens it would cost 'em a ruddy fortune!'

After their business in Zimbabwe had failed, and their lives had become so miserable that eventually she and her husband decided to separate, Christine had no option but to return to her parents' home at Alton, where she spent months fuming with frustration, unable to work, with two young children, and almost giving up hope of ever finding her own accommodation. Then, after she'd pestered them endlessly, a call had come through from the council. There was a house empty on an estate called Babs Field in the village of Bentley, would she be interested in looking at it?

'I looked around the house, and I thought, this is just magic. It was run down, the garden was over-grown, there hadn't been anyone living in it for four months, and it was February, when nothing looks at its best. But it meant independence after all these years, my own place. I just thought, this is fantastic.'

Inevitably, Christine soon bumped into Denise and Kevin, who also had twins. The two families became close, and, with Kevin's job secure, Christine and Denise became the best of friends.

Now things were improving fast: she had a car, she set about taming the garden with a hitherto unrecognised passion, and, with Denise's encouragement, she decided to apply for an access course at Guildford University which would lead to the science degree she'd always longed for.

'Why not go for it?' Denise asked.

'Why not indeed? I'm an optimist,' said Christine. 'I always have been, that's how I've survived.'

Michael and Norelle, the twins, were becoming excited about the Flower Show. They made necklaces of biscuits and beads for the craft show, and Christine took Michael out to agonise over his selection of violas.

'You're entering the class with the pansies and violas, aren't you? There are your violas, the ones you bought. Do you remember buying them?'

'No,' said Michael.

'Yes you do.'

'No I don't.'

'Yes you do. And look how they've grown, so many of them now.'

'Then there was just a couple, now they've grown lots and lots,' said Michael, suddenly remembering.

'We've got to have seven for your class in the Show, so you choose the best seven, and who knows, Michael, you might just win.'

Across on the cricket green, the Fête committee chairman David Asher was about to witness the annual miracle of the raising of the ancient marquee.

It was a magnificent sight, once up; a huge bell of a tent, given to the village in 1912, and the kind of structure Baden-Powell himself would have been impressed by, considering it ideal, no doubt, to house a legion of boy scouts on some great jungle expedition.

Over the years it had been endlessly patched and repaired, so that the mottled shades of canvas made it look almost as though it was camouflaged against the trees behind; and the rings that lined the base of the tent, where the peg ropes were secured and which took most of the strain when the wind got up, had been stitched so many times that the material around each ring was almost transparent.

David watched with a mixture of fascination and trepidation as the scoutmaster, Bob Wilson, gave the order to 'take ropes' and some of the lads from the Star he'd pressed into service prepared to take the strain.

'It's got to go up together, remember to go

together!' he yelled, and his voice echoed eerily across the green in the steamy evening air.

'Heave!'

There was a sudden cacophony of deep, heavy groans, and like a great beast rising from all fours, the marquee trembled, and began to reach for the sky, rolling crazily for a moment in a sudden gust of wind.

'End one OK . . . far side, stop!' shouted Bob. 'Stop, middle . . . this end, pull more!'

With one final, defiant lurch, the marquee was up, and David rushed into action with his sledgehammer, hammering down the iron pegs with all the strength in his body, as if that alone would ensure the marquee would remain standing until the end of the Show.

He had a feeling that after eighty years of invaluable service, this might be the year the marquee decided to bow out gracefully.

For a man who had flown hundreds of thousands of miles on oil business without so much as a second thought, John Dobson was looking decidedly agitated, as he joined a small band of anoraked travellers standing silently in a circle, waiting to climb into the hot-air balloon.

'You're enclosed in an aeroplane, you can't actually look down,' he said. 'And it's the looking down which makes me feel distinctly uncomfortable.' This was an idea that had been reinforced recently on the Eiffel Tower.

It was a warm, sparkling, sunny evening, yet there was a breeze, and all day John had been nervously looking out of his window at the Bentley and Froyle Oil Company, watching the tips of the trees bend, now slightly more, now slightly less.

'I haven't done any work at all today,' he said. 'People have been ribbing me about their terrible experiences of being in these things, how friends have come into the office in the morning ripped to pieces, having been dragged through trees, and so on. Apparently landing's much worse when there's a wind.'

The pilot walked over to him, looking at his watch, and then up again to the sky.

'Presumably it's more blowy up there than it is down here?' John asked him, rather hoping that the pilot would thank him for pointing out this fact, and suddenly call the trip off.

'Yes, the wind speed decreases in proportion to how near it gets to the ground – the friction of the earth slows it up. Where it's probably doing ten or twelve knots down here now, it's nearer fifteen or twenty knots at 2000 feet.'

'I wish you'd just bought me a tie, or a pair of underpants, like you normally do, dear,' he said to his wife, Janet.

'Are you really scared?'

'Just a bit.'

Just then the pilot start to address them.

'Would anyone who's flying please come over here,' he said, in that methodical, almost robotic tone pilots always adopt when about to take to the air.

=== TWENTY ===

From the air, the lake looked exactly as Hilda remembered it, a long, still, deep blue channel of water, as a big as a sea, and in the low sunlight sparkling so brightly that Livingstone had christened it in his log his 'lake of a thousand stars.'

To her left, Hilda could just make out the silhouette of the Livingstone Heights on the Mozambique side of the lake. In front stood the great Zomba plateau, towering over what had been the original capital, Blantyre, named after Livingstone's birthplace in Scotland; below and to her right, the endless green of the vast tobacco plantations that earn Malawi its only substantial foreign currency, interspersed with dozens of tiny circles, the mud-walled and thatched huts of the villages, where even today most of the population lives.

The 747 banked, and came gently in to land beside the modern, low-slung concrete and glass terminal buildings of Kamuzu International Airport, named after the man who'd declared himself Life President after Nyasaland became independent Malawi in 1964, Dr Hastings Kamuzu Banda.

In the 1950s it used to take Hilda three weeks to get out here, via the Suez Canal and Dar-Es-Salaam, but now the flight was less than ten hours, and the lake steamer was already on its way up the lake from Monkey Bay to meet her at Chilumba, only a few more hours drive up the coast.

Hilda had fond memories of the old *Ilala*. Built in Glasgow in 1949, the ship was taken out to Southern Africa, piece by piece, where it was reassembled on the shores of the lake. For many of the waterside villages, where no road has yet been able to penetrate, it remains a lifeline, with every inch of its second and third class decking crammed with villagers loaded down by boxes, bicycles, old sewing-machines, goats, chickens and thin-looking dogs.

Slightly to Hilda's disappointment, however, it wasn't the *Ilala* after all but her rather less romantic and more modern sister ship, the *Mtendere*, which was waiting to take her on the long journey down the lake.

Nevertheless, it was with a growing sense of excitement that Hilda sat in the prow of the launch taking her out to the ship anchored off the shore. Even in these choppy waters Hilda managed to time her leap from launch to ship with the practised eye of an old hand, although she had been grateful to feel the outstretched hands of the grinning crew grab her as she landed with a bump on deck.

'Thank you so much,' she said, straightening her hat, and wondering how much of the native Chiman' yanja she'd be able to remember over the next week.

The *Mtendere* was shuddering gently as the anchor chain was hauled up. Hilda eased her way through the throngs of chattering people lying and sitting on all the stairways, found her cabin, and stepped out into the intense sunlight to drink in her first considered view of the lake and waterside.

For a moment she felt faint with the heat. It was midday, and she stood with the sun directly overhead, completely shadowless.

If she'd feared the disappointment of anticlimax, she needn't have worried; it was as though at last she'd come home.

Later, Hilda was joined by a young Malawian university lecturer, travelling to Nkhotakota, and together they leant over the deck-rail as the ship began its long journey south, past the thin, winding tracks where groups of native women who'd just disembarked were heading off to the hills, casually bearing huge bags and boxes on their heads.

The man's name was Michael; as so often here, he'd been given one of the dozens of British Christian names that were the legacy of missionary colonisation; and his strong, youthful face expressed genuine interest as she eagerly told him about her past life.

'Do you know, on Likoma the native boys would come and ask me to swim with them, every Sunday, and every Sunday I readily agreed, rather pleased to have been asked. One day I said to them, it's very kind of you to invite me every week like this, and they said, not at all, we're happy to, because the crocodiles will always go for the white skin first, leaving us the chance to escape. Well! I wasn't so keen after that.

'As well as the *Ilala*, we used to travel a lot on an old wood-fired steamer, the *Chauncy Maples*.'

'The *Chauncy Maples* is still in service, Miss Evans.

It's now the oldest passenger ship still in use anywhere in the world.'

The *Chauncy Maples*, named after one of the two Anglican priests who first established a religious community on Likoma in 1886, had been built in 1901, although her wood-burning engines had long ago been replaced by oil.

'Oh, I do so hope we see it,' said Hilda.

'We might cross its path, down by Nkhotakota, Miss Evans.'

They looked across to the small rocky outcrops that climbed out of the water and up through the steep, green banks of trees that led up behind, a little thinner now than Hilda remembered, since wood was still the principal form of fuel and the trees in constant demand for dug-out canoes. Beyond stood the dark, brooding walls of the hills, broken only now and then by thin, gently-steaming waterfalls.

It was a sight that had hardly changed in thousands of years. In two days, Hilda would be stepping back on to the sands of Likoma Island itself, and even though she hadn't even seen a picture of the place in over thirty years, she had a shrewd suspicion that not much would have changed there, either.

Words had never sounded sweeter to the ears of John Dobson.

'I'm sorry to be the bearer of bad tidings,' said the pilot. 'But Gatwick are saying that although they've got a wind-speed down there of only five knots, it's still gusting up to between eight and ten knots, and if you're trying to land a large balloon and you get hit by a gust like that, anything could happen, you could fall out of the sky or finish up in a tree. We've waited as long as we dare. I'm afraid we are going to have to call it off.'

Most of the little group slouched with dis-appointment.

'I think it was worth getting you all here, on the off-chance it might improve, but I don't want to break anybody's neck, least of all my own.'

John was grinning like a Cheshire cat.

'What a shame!' said Janet.

'I think when he said it's better to be down here wishing you were up there, than up there wishing you were down here, I saw what he meant,' said John.

'Would have been exciting.'

'I certainly don't want to go up if it's dangerous.'

'You can forget about it now.'

'Until the day before we do it next time. Talk about prolonging the agony.'

'You look a bit more relaxed now.'

'I'm still badly in need of a drink.'

At first Tony thought it looked like some small mobile rocket-launcher, as the two men parked the Land Rover and tipped up the trailer so that the length of pipe was pointing almost vertically into the air.

He was joined by the parish clerk, Eric Hale, and together they wandered over slowly to the middle of the field, as the inner drill of the pipe started its regular, crashing thrusts, pushing deep down into the soil beneath Tony's land.

After half-a-dozen deeper and deeper thuds, the engine of the pipe was throttled back, and the point of the drill examined by one of the men, who put his finger

Over the hill by Glade Farm

into the three-inch hole and scraped out some soil samples.

'What's happened to your water-table, then, Mr Holmes?'

These were the bore-tests required by the surveyors drawing up the detailed specifications for the bypass, and the two engineers were surprised, and slightly puzzled, at the depth of the water-table; particularly since the proposed route took the new road within a hundred yards of the River Wey.

'It's been dropping dramatically over the last two years,' said Tony.

'How much rain should we have been having, Eric?'

'Our monthly average is two and half inches. But we've been getting less than a quarter of that over the last few months.'

'That new gauge the NRA have installed by Anstey Bridge to check the levels, that hasn't even registered, has it?'

'The water hasn't even reached the bottom marker.'

'River hasn't been this low for donkeys' years.'

'At Alton, the river's dry,' said Eric. 'Do you know, that brewery there is working twenty-four hours a day now, producing one and a quarter million pints of beer every single day. That must have an effect.'

'A million and a quarter pints?'

'Then there's the pumping out to Basingstoke. It's only those streams coming down from the hills at Holybourne that is giving us any water at all. It's so sluggish at the bottom of my garden, it's completely weeding up,' said Eric, who used to write the 'Nature Notes' column for the *Farnham Herald*.

'What we need is a damn good flush out.'

The island children were fighting for a place at the water's edge, some actually falling in as the sheer weight of the crowd behind pushed them forwards.

It always seemed a party when the lake steamer came to Likoma, bearing on the decks everything on which an island community depended for its survival. Now the *Mtendere* was edging around the headland, and into the gently-lapping waves of the bay, with a fleet of dug-out canoes heading out to greet her, the thin, dark blades of the paddles flashing quickly in the sun.

Hilda was in the first boat, crammed into the bow, waving at the sea of smiling faces that grew ever larger. The boat juddered into the sand, and Hilda was pitched forward, before standing in a rather wobbly way, and leaping into the mass of bodies. It seemed as if the entire island had turned out to greet her. Behind the sea of smiling, cheering faces, a phalanx of more than a hundred schoolchildren had formed up neatly as part of the official welcoming ceremony. As Hilda scrambled ashore they began to chant 'We're so happy, we're so happy to see you again!'

There on the shore was Peter Tuntuwa, a vast grin plastered from ear to ear; at a distance, in his dog-collar and black cassock, he looked just as she remembered him as a young priest, but as she drew nearer, Hilda noticed the lines on his face and grey flecks in his short curly hair.

Not that it mattered one jot, of course; they held hands, and smiled; and then there was Stanley, and Eric and Michael, and the village chiefs, their arms thrown around her shoulders, hurrying her up the hill to the old school hall, with its warped and splintered timbers, where she had so often addressed her pupils.

In fact, the village had changed, just a little. Money from a German aid programme had meant that some of the mud huts had been replaced by brick buildings, still a rare sight outside the towns; and the huge cathedral, where she had often prayed and where the door to the belfry remained locked then, as now, so the bats could rest undisturbed in the heat of the day, had a shining new corrugated iron roof.

Up at the hall, there were great speeches of welcome and dozens of little gifts from the villagers. It was almost as if the Queen herself had arrived.

Later she walked with Peter into the cool of the cathedral, which still boasts carvings from the Bavarian Alps, bricks from Canterbury, soil under the altar from Jerusalem, and a cross from Zambia made from a tree that had grown beside the spot where Livingstone's heart is buried. Hilda slowly looked round and tried to take in every detail, every emotion, to soak her memory with it all, for at that moment she realised that this was her last opportunity: she would never have the chance to return here again.

Tony and Eric may have wanted six inches of rain to wash away the weeds on the dried-out banks of the Wey, but for most of the rest of the villagers, particularly members of both Fête and Flower Show committees, tomorrow of all days needed to be dry.

In kitchens, on street corners, over garden fences, the weather was the only topic of conversation that evening, and at Well Cottage, by the church, David Asher and his wife Clare were huddled over the radio, listening nervously for the forecast, unable quite to grasp the possibility that in the middle of one of the worst droughts for years, the Show could end up a wash-out.

'The weather looks quite unsettled this weekend,

with showers or longer spells of rain,' droned a voice from the BBC Weather Centre. 'It's also going to turn increasingly cool and windy.'

David and Clare looked at each other in silence for a moment.

'We may be lucky,' said David, at length. 'If the wind doesn't freshen too much, the bad weather won't come through too quickly. That means we might get it Sunday rather than Saturday, which might mean problems getting the marquee down.'

'Especially if it's windy as well as wet.'

'But a dry Saturday would be wonderful.'

TWENTY-ONE

At dawn, not even the old cock down at Bury Court bothered to rise out of bed. The sound of the rain was enough, a constant, ceaseless hammering, on roofs, on pathways and fields, and, rather more importantly, on the cricket pitch down by School Lane, where once again squadrons of ducks were circulating in anticipation of a spot of midsummer scuba-diving, and the old marquee sagged under the weight of the pools forming where the belltop met the canvas walls.

'I could have told 'em this would happen, Jack,' said old Walter to his long-standing friend and gardening club committee member, Jack Wiltshire.

'How so, Walter?'

'You should have heard those trains a-rattlin' down to Alton last night,' said Walter. 'Never heard anything like it.'

Jack had called into Toad Hole Lane to collect Walter's roses in his car. Walter had them ready, of course, in a big silver bucket in the parlour.

'Oh Walter, they're wonderful,' said Jack.

'They've been good this year.'

'There are some marvellous ones already down the marquee,' said Jack. 'Put mine to shame, they do.'

'I'll be down a little later this afternoon, Jack, after Jessie and I have done our shift on the gate at Jenkyn Place. We were expecting a fair few today, but now I'm not so sure.'

'Righty-oh, Walt, see you later. Take care now.'

By mid-morning, the bar of the Star was full, this time with members of another village team undergoing a vital tactics talk. They were the Star Bale-Throwing Side, getting tanked up in preparation for the traditional bloodthirsty competition between local pubs, which usually ends up with the teams throwing bales at each other, instead of over the carefully measured course. Trevor, the landlord, had artfully secured the services of Big Pete and his chums by bribing them away from the Social Club Side with the offer of free drinks.

'That Hopblossom was a pretty good team last year,' said Pete, his formidable frame perched precariously on the edge of a bar-stool.

'The Prince of Wales are usually quite good.'

'Nah, we stuffed 'em last year!'

The Hopblossom, a pub in Farnham, were the current holders. The previous year one pub's contingent had disgraced themselves by arriving at the Show in a lorry which had been driven the wrong way down the dual carriageway. It had parked, rather needlessly with hindsight, right beside the Hampshire Constabulary stand; the driver had climbed out of the lorry, fallen flat on his face, and was promptly arrested.

'Want another drink, Pete?'

'Yea, I've had two pints already. By half-past two,

I reckon we'll all have had another four each, and then we'll be ready to go for it!'

'Right!'

'By the end of the day, we'll be on fifteen or sixteen.'

'Right!'

'Well, it only happens once a year, don't it?'

By noon, the rain had eased, although the wind was increasing, and David Asher, having seen the ladies at the cake stall trying to catch the wrapping-paper flying off like kites from their produce and the Indian Arts and Crafts table actually roll over, was pacing nervously around the flaps of the marquee, scrutinising the canvas for early signs of strain.

The children's band had arrived in a large bus, and were unloading their huge brass instruments, many of which seemed larger than the musicians.

David had suggested they position the music stands in a large arc, facing out towards the field from the front of the pavilion, close to the public lavatories.

'Your music's going to be blowing all over the place, isn't it?' asked David, envisaging a nightmare scene where thirty-five music sheets of *Seventy-Six Trombones* lifted off as one, heading for the south coast.

The conductor of the children's band prided himself on his long experience of playing at such events, and had taken suitable precautions.

'My wife hasn't got any pegs at all at home to hang the washing out, because they're all here,' he said, walking around the children like Father Christmas, inviting them each to take a clothes-peg from his huge bag, to secure their music on to the stands.

Lady Davie, the widow of Sir Paul Davie from the Old Rectory who died last year, had agreed to open the

Show, and she arrived now, clad in a heavy raincoat and waterproof hat, under the attendant escort of the president of the Show Committee, Lieutenant-General Sir William Pike, carefully stepping over the puddles.

'Welcome, welcome,' said David Asher, guiding her towards the front of the bale-throwing arena, where the bunting was flapping madly in the growing wind.

'Testing, one-two-three, testing!' announced the lady who'd wired the microphone.

'There may be a problem with the electrics, it may even be a power cut,' she said, ominously. 'I've only lived in Bentley for four years but the village is renowned for its power cuts, isn't it?'

'Is there a power cut now?'

'I'm not sure, because the Bouncy Castle has just collapsed. It was up, but now it's down, and looking a bit sad.'

Suddenly the microphone burst into life, the Bouncy Castle started to reflate, and after a short introduction by Sir William, Lady Davie began her opening address, much of which was inaudible, carried away from the main arena by the breeze.

'Can everybody hear me?' said Lady Davie, slightly forlornly, but as she spoke, the sun burst through the cloud, and a small cheer rose up from those listening close around her.

'Welcome to everybody here today. We run the Fête to supply the money to pay for all the good causes in Bentley. To keep the roof on the Memorial Hall. To mend the sports pavilion which was vandalised by the people it was built for . . .'

'Right children, check your pegs!' said the bandmaster, under his breath.

'So I have great pleasure in declaring the Fête open!'

A polite ripple of applause moved through those few standing at the front of the crowd who had caught what Lady Davie had said.

'We're starting with *Holly Hedges*, Judith,' said the bandmaster. 'As I have already said, straight in, as usual.'

A small girl behind a huge euphonium was frantically trying to unstick a valve.

'Hurry up, Helen.'

The crowd was expectant, waiting for something to happen.

'Just leave it for now, Helen, and peg up *Holly Hedges.*'

Another girl started waving at someone in the crowd.

'Emma, pay attention, never mind what's happening around you, keep your eyes on the music.'

'What are we starting with again?'

'*Holly Hedges*, Emma. After three.'

The music seemed to be a signal for people to relax, and begin drifting around the stalls. By now, parts of the field were in danger of becoming positively marshy, as the blinding sun quickly burnt off the surface water, turning it into steamy mud. Nobody seemed to mind. For a time Jim Harden was front-runner in the wellie-wanging; beside the 'Pluck-a-Hen' stall, Edy Parrot, her Royal correspondence safely secure inside her handbag, where she always kept it when not at home, was launching a powerful broadside at the coconuts; and there was the redoubtable Mrs Morris, leading the applause for the Bentley School Maypole Dancing team.

Clare, a three-year-old Jersey Hereford cross, had just arrived. She belonged to Dave Hunt, the village milkman, and now the huge brown freckled hands which could cheerfully carry a milk bottle on each finger were gently massaging the animal's great haunches, in an attempt to coax her out of the back of the box, and into a special section of grass cordoned off at the far end of the field.

This was the star of Bentley's famous Cowpat Lottery, and already there was queue of people waiting to pay a pound to secure a two-foot square of the grass at which Clare was now contentedly munching away, in the hope that she might soon deign to perform on it, and thus secure the tenant the grand first prize of two hundred and fifty pounds.

'Mightn't we have to wait all afternoon?' asked one newcomer.

Dave slowly turned and gave the enquirer the withering look of a man who didn't have the temper to waste time explaining country ways to heathens. 'On average, a cow craps once an hour,' he said at last, his eyes bulging and rolling like a pantomime Long John Silver.

'She 'asn't been since before noon. Any moment now and 'er booells will explode, you mark my words.'

Old Walter had arrived at last, after his stint at Jenkyn Place, and was immediately up there with the best of them, waving his pound in the air.

'Nothing like this in my day,' he said, with obvious admiration.

'We don't mark out the actual field,' said Ken, the computer expert who was the mastermind behind the technical detail of the Cowpat Lottery. 'You choose a square on my computer sheet here, which represents the area where Clare is.'

'I see,' said Walter, looking a little confused.

'Supposing the cow plops just here,' said Ken,

jabbing a finger at the middle of the paper. 'The angle here is fifty-two degrees, so the distance along is forty-four feet, cosine fifty-two, which makes it twenty-seven feet along from the corner; and on the other way we need to take fifty-two, sine it this time, by four-four, and that gives us thirty-four feet exactly.'

'I see,' said Walter.

Big Pete and the boys from the Star were lumbering up to the bale-throwing arena, just in time for the first heat, still wiping their mouths on their sleeves, and grabbing bales.

'Right, the Hopblossom, the defenders of this great title, are about to throw their first bale!' screamed Giles Harrap down the microphone, his voice, so much more familiar in the tranquil setting of the Crown Court, now deafening those standing within fifty yards of the loudspeakers.

'Will the Harrap children please get out of the way!'

Suddenly people were diving for cover as a large bale winged its way dangerously close to the perimeter rope.

'It's a great throw for the Hopblossom!'

The Star, not surprisingly to anyone who'd known how long they'd spent at tactics talk, initially put in a rather mediocre performance, although it didn't seem to dent Pete's determination, partly because he'd already downed eight pints, and at least four cans.

'I reckon we're heading for a confident second at the minute,' he said. 'But it could be a first. We've had to lend the Hopblossom one of our players.'

'You can't even see the bale, let alone throw it!' said one of the crowd.

'I don't have to throw it, I'm the Captain!'

In the marquee, Walter was being interviewed by the Press.

'Hello Mr Sherfield, Annette Booth, village correspondent for the *Farnham Herald*.'

'Afternoon to you!'

'What do you think of the Show this year?'

'I think the flowers look very good, despite the problems with the weather. I haven't been around the vegetables yet, but the flowers certainly look wonderful. I don't know whether you heard, but I met Alan Titchmarsh a few weeks back. He well remembered my herbaceous borders, up at Jenkyn Place.'

Walter was asked to pose for a picture, holding the legendary Baden-Powell Cup for Best in Show. He had won it three times in succession back in the fifties, and after that had been asked to stand down to let others have a chance.

'Presented to the Bentley Flower Show, by Lady Baden-Powell, for the competition, in commemoration of having lived in Bentley for twenty-five years, in the year 1938,' read the words engraved on the cup. The first holder was presented with it in 1939, Mr A. Smith.

'Do you remember old Arthur Smith, Walter?'

'Lived in Babs Field, the porter down at the station. Rare grower.'

'And what's this one here?'

'That's the Dick Holmes cup,' said Walter. 'For the best bowl of hybrid tea roses. Dick Holmes was Tony Holmes' father, of course.'

As soon as the rain had stopped, and the sun burst through, Tony rang up Eric Hale and asked him if he had time to meet again, down on Tony's fields beyond the main road.

'Seen those pegs, Eric, that've sprouted up overnight? Can't make head nor tail of 'em!'

They met by Vickory Cottages, on the track down to where Mrs Coke's son John had started a nursery at Bentley Green Farm. In front of them, about twenty yards away, were two pine posts; they could see another pair at the end of the field, by the track which ran up to the hop-pickers' huts; and two more, away in the distance, up by the main road to the west of the village.

'These pegs are the first physical signs of the bypass we've seen here, since before the War,' said Tony. 'And I think they ought to be put in a museum, and kept for posterity.'

'Might start growing into trees if they wait as long again.'

'Do those pegs mark the width of the thing, Eric? Can't be!'

'No, they're just showing the alignment. Look I'll show you.'

Eric went to his car, and returned bearing two huge scrolls of paper.

'I've got the biggest and best maps there are,' said Eric. 'They don't come bigger.'

He spread the maps over the front of the Range Rover.

'You should have got a bigger car, the maps are bigger than the car.'

'Farmers can't afford big cars any more.'

'Here it goes, Tony, off the Farnham bypass, cutting through between Marelands and Marelands Lodge, just north of the sewage works, and past right here where we're standing, that's what the pegs are there for, showing the slight bend in the road.'

'Then off in front of John Coke's house, Bentley Green Farm – his view's going to change, isn't it? – and back down to the main road again.'

'That's it.'

Tony took a long, deep, breath, staring hard at the pegs which in a few months would start to be transformed into tarmac. The sheer scale of the project was starting to sink in.

'Easier to visualise now, somehow.'

'It's really going to happen.'

'Going out to contract soon.'

On the far side of the field, they could see the cars and lorries on the main road, speeding past the War Memorial Hall.

'That's why it's taken so long,' said Eric. 'There's no major congestion through the village, the traffic is flowing most of the time, and that's the way they judge it. Unlike Alresford, for example. There used to be a solid block of traffic there for miles, do you remember? So they got their bypass.'

'Historic day for the village, this,' said Tony, unable to take his eyes off the pegs. 'I'm just sorry that a lot of the people who really initiated the thing to start with, won't see it. They're too old, now.'

'This has really become one of the high points of village life, hasn't it?' said the Revd Bill Rogers, sipping tea with Margaret Evans outside the pavilion, and wondering if he stood a chance of winning a prize by guessing correctly how many balloons there were stuffed into a car parked on the grass beside them.

'Well, it gets everyone working together, doesn't it, and there's such a tremendous team on the committee now. Of course, there's Froyle Show next week, and Binsted the week after, so you're going to be busy, Bill.'

'All part of a day's work,' said Mr Rogers. 'I've got my eye on that superb terracotta garden pot in the raffle. You've found some good prizes this year.'

'Yes, we've got a pair of tickets to the Redgrave Theatre in Farnham as well, and a free hairdo at the Village Stores,' said Margaret.

'How marvellous.'

Giles Harrap was almost uncontrollable with excitement, as the bale-throwing entered its final phase.

'This is the last throw, and it's a real biggie for the Prince of Wales!' he cried, his voice hoarse with the afternoon's exertions.

'It's a winner, a winner, a winner!'

Pete, who was having trouble standing, looked dejected.

'Well, at least we've come in third, although we should have done better, shouldn't we lads?'

'You weren't third, you were fourth!'

'No we weren't!'

'We were third. Hopblossom second, and Social Club first. You were fourth!'

'OK, so we were fourth!'

It was remarkable that the marquee was still standing, thought David Asher, as once again he patrolled the edge of the canvas, now beginning to tear beyond repair after the afternoon's buffeting. Next year, he'd really have to bring to an end that little piece of village history, and insist a new marquee be bought.

'Tremendous gate, David,' said Richard Leonard, the treasurer. 'Over a thousand people.'

Inside the gently swaying tent, General Sir William Pike was announcing the winners of the Flower and Vegetable Classes.

'The Winner of the Mrs Coke Cup – none other than the secretary of our Flower Show Committee, Sara Deane!' he said. Miss Deane stepped forward amid cheers, and took the cup from Lady Davie, still clad in her waterproofs despite the sun. 'Clearly a popular choice,' he added.

'Certificates of Merit for Produce go to Mrs Joan Thomas for her chutney,' continued Sir William, 'And Mrs Westcott for her Victoria sponge!'

Lady Davie picked up the great Baden-Powell Cup, and a hush fell on the crowd.

'And the Lady Baden-Powell Cup For most Points In The Show goes to . . .' The General paused for a moment, to gain maximum effect. 'It goes to our parish clerk and his wife, Mr and Mrs Eric Hale!'

Eric was grinning wildly, and he waved his arm in the air, like an Olympic salute, as he received the prized trophy from Lady Davie.

The applause, from such a small crowd, was considerable.

'Three cheers for Lady Davie!' said Sir William. 'Hip-hip! Hooray!'

Christine and the twins emerged from the marquee, looking tired, but well pleased. They bumped into Kevin and Denise, and their twins.

'How did you get on?' asked Denise.

'I got a first for the fruit cake, which I was really thrilled about, and Norelle got a second prize for her necklace, and Michael got a highly commended for his violas!'

'Well done!'

'I've loved it! We've had such a good day, haven't we Michael?'

From the other side of the field came a huge cheer, and a group of people were running toward a large, dark pile of steaming dung.

Clare had done her duty, at least for another year.

TWENTY-TWO

In the last few weeks of the summer, rush-hour drivers on the main A31 Farnham to Alton road were meeting unaccustomed delays on what everyone, particularly the road-planners, knew to be a fast-moving section of road, through the village of Bentley.

Every morning at about seven-thirty, a tall young man with long blond hair, wearing stained old jeans and a tatty shirt, would step out boldly into the middle of the road, and wave down the traffic to a stop, whilst an elderly lady in a battery-powered three-wheeled buggy inched slowly across from one side to the other, giving a little aristocratic wave to the drivers, not unlike the Queen Mother.

Some were intrigued; other drivers, perhaps late for work, cursed; when was this place going to get a bypass? On one occasion, somebody had the temerity to give the three-wheeler a blast with their horn, and the elderly lady gave another, more specific gesture, quite unlike the Queen Mother.

In the evening, at about five o'clock, the ritual was

reversed, the only difference this time being that both the young man and the elderly lady were by this stage in the day covered in twigs and bits of leaf, which the more knowledgeable would immediately have recognised as emanating from the humble hop-vine.

Nobody had been sure if Ada Allen would appear for hop-picking this year, after her heart-attack; nobody, that is, except Ada herself, who had managed to wring the three-wheeler from the Social Services Department at her home at Manor Park, E12, and had persuaded her grandson Chris to drive it down with her. Without it, she'd have been unable to get from her hut (still without electricity) across to her throne on the hop-picking machine.

'Oh you look beautiful, you lovely girl!' Tony said when he first saw her. 'You look beautiful on your hot-rod here, your Ferrari!'

'It isn't a Ferrari, Tony, it's an invalid three-wheeler, just to help get me about. I'm perfectly all right, Tony, it's just my ruddy legs, and I'm getting old, and decrepit and I can only walk a short distance at a time.'

'You don't use that to drive across the main road, surely?'

'I do!' said Ada. 'I just don't care!'

'Stop, stop the traffic!' said Tony, almost crying with laughter.

'Stop the lot, Ada's coming!'

'You've heard of Supergran, you ought to see me fly across that road!'

'And when we've got the caravan fixed up, you can pull it behind!'

'Just so long as you keep letting me charge up the batteries, Tony. And when I pass my driving test I'm going to get a Porsche!'

'You'll deserve a Roller by then!'

'Ain't he nasty?'

Everyone at Glade Farm had been surprised at how fit Ada had looked, apart from her legs giving out, and how nimble still were her fingers.

'I never could die young, Tony, I'm all right 'till about two hundred. Now, what about my house down here?'

I t looked at though it would be a good hop crop this summer. With overall temperatures lower than last year, the red spider had been less apparent, and easier to conquer. The unit of measure for dried hops is the zentner, or 50 kilos, and Chris Holmes had told his father to expect over 800 zentners, a big improvement, of which all but eighty would be grade One.

In the kitchen at Glade Farm, Tony was deep into his *Pedigree Dexter Journal* when a pale Pom appeared, yawning and stretching.

'You're like a motor-car in the mornings. Short of fuel,' said Tony.

'Motor-car?'

'Need stoking up with food to get you started.'

'Oh.'

'Pom, do you mind going down to the shed today?' said Tony. 'Give the pickers their cash?'

'I don't mind,' said Pom, trooping off with a large mug of coffee.

'She'll do something, one day, will Pom,' said Tony, when Maureen arrived. 'She's a tough cookie, you don't ride over her, that's for sure. If you cross her, she bites! And why not? She's all right!'

After breakfast, Tony drove down to Bury Court

to see Bob Bates, his former cattleman. At last he had some good news. The second gardener at Jenkyn Place was leaving, and Mrs Coke had offered Bob the job.

'I'm not much good at gardening, but perhaps that won't matter much, I can do as I'm told,' said Bob.

'You'll be on the television soon, presenting *Gardeners' World*.'

'Suits me a treat, really. It means I can stay here.'

'That's the worst thing, the upheaval of moving.'

'Good thing. Still be able to go up the Cedars with the boys on Friday night.'

'Still be able to go beating for the guns.'

'Wife'll be pleased.' Bob is married to Daisy Cox's daughter Marion.

'After forty years, though, I'll miss the cattle.'

'Worst day's work I've ever done, having to get rid of you, Bob, but there it is, that's life I'm afraid. Sign of the times.'

Bob said nothing for a moment.

'We thought we were sailing so beautifully – then all of a sudden, boing! It's happened. Sara dying. Death duties. There you are. It happens!'

'I'd still like to go and see the herd, Mr Holmes, up at that prison in Rugby.'

'We'll go, Bob, one day.'

Tony drove back towards Hole Lane, down past the empty cattle-sheds.

'If I was really brave,' he said to Chris, 'If I was really brave, in a few years' time, I wouldn't mind starting up the show-herd again.'

After using the office screen to watch England put in a creditable bowling performance after a hopeless first innings of only two hundred and three, on an admittedly damp, grassy wicket, John Dobson spent most of the day on the telephone to Lagos, speaking to the Nigerian National Petroleum Corporation.

Even by his standards, this was a tight corner. He had just received confirmation that 900,000 barrels of Nigerian crude had been loaded on to his client's ship at what today's teletext clearly showed him to be a price about half a million dollars less than they'd paid for it. That was the gamble in signing a fixed-price contract four weeks in advance of purchase. Sometimes you won.

'Half a million, could be a bit more, could be less,' he said, to a slightly concerned client on the other side of the Atlantic. 'Until we actually get rid of it, we won't know its precise value.'

Now they had to make more decisions; should the Bentley and Froyle Oil Company sell the cargo at such a loss to one of the big oil companies, like Shell or BP; or should they stick with it, refine it into gasoline or jet fuel, and hope to make more by selling off the products one by one?

Half a million dollars, all in one day!

That was the kind of news more easily digested after a soothing consultation with George Farquharson, the master of the Rum Toft, up at the Prince of Wales.

Tony drove down Hole Lane, and left opposite Jenkyn Place. He had seen Mrs Coke the other day, and she'd been cock-a-hoop. She had been given a new young cedar, no more than four feet high, to replace the grand old tree which had stood on the East Front since 1823, and which came crashing down the week after her husband died.

'It won't look any good at all until long after I've gone, of course,' she said to Tony. 'But it is rather a nice thing to have, don't you think? I shan't plant it in quite the same place, though. Where do you think it should go?'

Tony went slowly along School Lane, and paused for a moment before turning right onto the main road, trying to visualise what the new bypass would look like as it veered off to the south just beyond Marelands Lodge. It was still hard to imagine.

He drove past the Village Stores, past the drive which led down to the old garage of the Bentley Motor Company and the Bentley and Froyle Oil Company, on past the Police House, where PC Goude was currently spearheading an investigation into a series of mysterious thefts involving the disappearance of no less than thirteen lawn-mowers in the village, including the new cricket-mower; and then he turned right at the crossroads, and up past the War Memorial Hall.

Tony drew up just in front of Babs Field, and parked, the engine still running. He was in no hurry. Workmen were swarming over the new building site; some of the houses were already up to roof-level. There had been a heated discussion at the parish council meeting about what the new housing estate should be called. The developers had named it 'Pipers Field', but that was only temporary, for the benefit of the sales staff. Somebody had suggested Quinta Close, because it stood behind the Quinta nursing home; someone else, Hole Estate.

Hole Estate!

'We've already got "Babs Field", and "Eggars Field", named after the Eggar family – why on earth don't we call it "Bonners' Field",' Tony argued. 'After

Harvey and Cath Bonner, of course. Over the years they've done so much for the village.'

So that's what it is to be called – Bonners' Field, in honour of the two people who delivered the mail in the village for so many years, and who between them only had six days off through ill health.

'Tea-break, my Lords, Ladies, and Gentlemen!' announced Brian Wilkins, switching off the hop-picking machine.

'Chris, here are your wages! Now, where's Ada?'

'Hello Pom!'

'Ada! How are you?'

'Lovely to be back amongst friends.'

Pom found Ada sitting in her usual place, where these days she remained during the tea-breaks, a conveyor-belt of cups of tea linking her to the teapot in the drying-shed.

'Any romance yet, Pom?'

'No, I'm too busy here, running round paying you lot!'

'It would be nice,' said Ada. 'We keep saying, I wonder if Pom's married?'

'No, no,' said Pom, laughing. 'Not for a long time, Ada, I've got too much to do before I settle down.'

'What you got to do, then Pom?'

'I'm just here for another week, until the end of the picking, and then I'm off to Israel for a week – '

'Israel? You do get about, don't you?'

'Then back to Oxford, for the last year of my degree.'

'Looking forward to it?'

'It'll be hard, the last year, settling down to

academic work after my year with the UN, no evenings free, no weekends. It's going to be a big shock, going back to all that.'

'Oh my. Then what?'

'I don't know. Something. But whatever happens, I expect I'll be back here for hop-picking next year, don't you worry, Ada.'

Ada couldn't take her eyes off Pom, as she moved about the shed, smiling, chatting, handing out the packets of cash; always so full of energy.

'She's her Mum,' said Ada. 'She really is her Mum, her speech, her mannerisms. She's a chip off the old block, is Pom.

'It's been hard for them this last year. Mrs Pike wrote to me and told me what had happened. It was Tony I was worried about, I thought, oh my God, what would happen? I was lost for words, Sara was so great, but seeing Pom, she's sort of re-living Sara. She's her mother's daughter.

'A couple of years ago, Pom was working with us, and it rained continuously, and she really lost her temper, our Pom. She said words I never expected from a lady. Well, as I looked up, and heard her, I laughed, so when we were outside, I had to apologise. I weren't laughing at you, Pom, I said, but it's just that you're like a chip off the old block! She said, that's all right Ada, no offence taken. She's a great person. Well, they're a great family, aren't they?'

The taxi bringing a deeply suntanned Hilda back from Heathrow drove over the hill by Glade Farm, and there, stretched out gloriously before her in the evening sun, was the valley, a delicate haze of mist

suspended above it, with the old semaphore tower sil-
houetted on the hill above Alice Holt forest, and the sun
glinting on the weathervane of St Mary's newly-roofed
bell-tower.

It may not have been quite so dramatic a scene as
the Zomba Plateau or the Manchewe Falls, but it was
home, and in the breeze that blew in through the rear
window of the car Hilda could detect that rich mixture
of countryside smells that could only be from this part
of Hampshire.

The holiday was over, there was work to be done.
Margaret had dreamed up another brilliant fund-
raising idea: a 'hymnathon', sponsored hymn-singing
in the church. How much money could they raise, she
wondered, if even half the village pledged money for the
choir to sing one hundred hymns non-stop?

There was no time to lose. Bishop Colin would be
here for the Flower Festival before they knew it.

EPILOGUE

After fifty years, the bypass has at last been built. For weeks afterwards people living by the old A31 couldn't sleep because it was so quiet. For the first time in generations you can park outside the shop, which has further revived Alan Wheatley's fortunes – he's now opening a teashop.

The shop delivery man, Terry Cox, has retired and the delivery service confined to history. Terry's thrown himself into the annual task of producing the most enormous carrots to be grown anywhere in Hampshire.

Sadly Old Walter Sherfield, Margaret Evans and Mrs Coke have died – Jenkyn Place has been sold. Hilda now runs the village Girl Guides' group and is contemplating another trip back to Malawi.

After travelling to nearly every corner of the globe, Pom has settled in Chicago where she's working for a publishing company.

Ada's never been in better health and still picks hops and dreams of Tony giving her a farm cottage in the village.

Catherine is now grown-up and after years of waiting for her belly-button has finally decided that the absence of one is much more interesting than having one, and is happy to remain belly-buttonless.

Tony Holmes has become a grandfather. Chris married a hotelier's daughter from Llandudno, Sarah, and produced a daughter, Olivia. Tony has eased himself painlessly into retirement, and passes his days contentedly fishing, playing golf with his brother-in-law Jumbo, and being interviewed by film crews.

John Nettles' Jersey

A personal history of the people and places, heroines, heroes and villains

John Nettles, BBC TV's Bergerac, delves deep into Jersey's past to reveal the island's colourful history. He records its prehistoric origins, its centuries'-long role as an outpost of England and some of the darker periods in Jersey's history – most recently, the five long years it suffered under German rule during the Second World War.

He highlights some of the fascinating characters born on the island, such as Lillie Langtry, the 'Jersey Lily', whose beauty brought her fame, fortune and the love of a prince. Finally, in keeping with his role as Jersey's fictional police-man, John Nettles describes some of the murders, solved and unsolved, that have bloodied the island's soil.

Woman's Hour Book of Short Stories

Selected and introduced by Pat McLoughlin

This volume brings together eighteen of the best stories by women writers featured on Radio 4's Woman's Hour. Their theme is 'aspects of love' in the broadest sense, the first innocent awakenings of desire rubbing shoulders with a more mature, sometimes harrowing, kind of love. The collection includes work by novelists from the recent past and leading contemporary writers.

A Hack in the Borders

Along the Offa's Dyke Path
Dylan Winter

One summer Dylan Winter sets out to travel along the
famous Offa's Dyke path through the English/Welsh border
country. This is his honest and amusing account of his
journey through countryside steeped in 2000 years of cross-
border feuding and countless legends and ghost stories. He
encounters Franciscan friars, off-beat archaeologists and
sentimental hill farmers on a path that leads to ancient hill
forts, gothic Victorian mansions and the occasional public
house.